Lucky to Live Here

YOUR GUIDE TO LIFE
IN THE YOSEMITE MOUNTAIN AREA

by
Kellie Flanagan
and
Jennifer Moss

LUCKY TO LIVE HERE: YOUR GUIDE TO LIFE IN THE
YOSEMITE MOUNTAIN AREA

CONTENTS

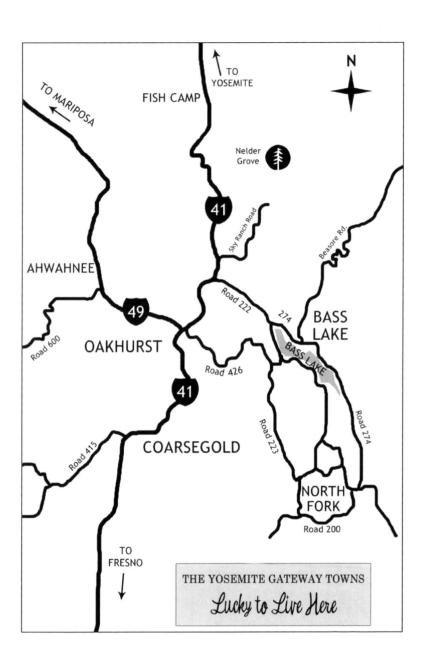

INTRODUCTION

From the time our daughter was a baby, almost twenty years ago, we'd pile into the car and make the five-hour drive from southern California to Bass Lake, then unwind at one of the many recreational sites reserved for campers. We would wake to the sounds of the forest, glassy water gleaming in the early light, smelling the intoxicating scent of pine and cedar trees as the sun began to shine. This is when I fell in love with the foothills of the central Sierra Nevada.

Having grown up at the beach I've swallowed my fair share of seawater. The contrasting calm, beautiful lake and its surroundings seemed the perfect place to vacation, away from the tall buildings, heavy traffic, and thronging masses. Vacations are, unfortunately, temporary and our smiles faded as we drove away from the mountains, back to our stressful urban existence. We wondered if we had the formula backwards. Perhaps, instead of spending our short vacation time pitching a tent in the beautiful Sierra, we could flip the script. Shouldn't we live where we loved to play?

When the time came to move, we found a realtor in the mountains and soon a house, and ten weeks after deciding to split the city, we were once again "camped out," this time in our five-bedroom home situated on nearly five acres. We've never regretted the move. – *Kellie Flanagan*

Twenty-some years ago I sat in my cubicle, one of many worker bees on the 43rd floor of an L.A. skyscraper. I stared at my computer screensaver as idyllic images glided by, from a lush green forest to a majestic waterfall to a ridge of snow-capped mountains. I wondered if these places truly existed—watching and yearning as my bucket list grew longer with each photograph.

Fast forward to current day, and now I see those same vistas when I look out of my own windows. Every day I think how lucky I am to live here in the Yosemite area. If you're reading this book then perhaps you are considering a big move: a move to the mountains. Maybe you're ready for retirement or you've just had enough of the city's noise, traffic, and human congestion. We've put together this guide because we've both gone through the move—from a bustling metropolis to the not-so-bustling mountain towns near one of the most beautiful national parks in the United States.

Moving to the mountains changed my life for the better, and achieving the dream wasn't as difficult as I thought it would be. This book grew out of a lunch conversation where Kellie and I were laughing at all the things we "city mice" had to learn after moving to the mountains. We hope in the following chapters we can help you with all the information we've found. – *Jennifer Moss*

WHAT THIS BOOK COVERS

Lucky to Live Here: Your Guide to Life in the Yosemite Mountain Area will provide you all of the information we wish we'd had upon moving here. In this book, we'll guide you through the planning, the move, and the adjustment of going from the city to the mountains and what you can expect in every phase. We'll cover searching for a home, mountain culture, activities, nightlife, wildlife, family life, business life, schools and more.

Believe it or not we uncovered treasures and information that we didn't even know before researching this book. There are so many fun things to do and people to meet in the Yosemite gateway communities, we hope this will be a useful guide to get started on your journey.

WHAT THIS BOOK IS NOT

This book is not intended to be a visitor's guide to Yosemite. It does not include hiking trails or detailed attractions in Yosemite National Park. We also chose not to include local business listings, as they are apt to change.

CHAPTER 1
Our Mountain Towns

The Yosemite mountain communities can seem like the small town ideal that you've see in old movies and television: as quaint as Mayberry in *The Andy Griffith Show*, as quirky as Cicely in *Northern Exposure*, or as comedic as Hooterville in *Green Acres*. Whatever your comparison, it certainly won't be anything like life in the city...we guarantee it.

What we call the Yosemite Gateway towns are established communities nestled near and around the southern entrance of Yosemite National Park, located in eastern Madera County in California.

Ahwahnee – a town approximately four miles from the center of Oakhurst up highway 49. The name Ahwahnee comes from a Miwok word which means "mouth." According to L.H. Bunnell's 1892 book, *Discovery of the Yosemite*, The Miwok named the Yosemite Valley "Ahwahnee" because it resembled the gaping mouth of a bear. Nipinnawasse, which translates to "plenty of deer," is a section of Ahwahnee off of Highway 49 and Road 601 with approximately 200 homes and several B&Bs.

Bass Lake – the collection of homes on and around the lake of the same name, east of Highway 41 and Oakhurst. The man-made lake is approximately four miles long and a half-mile wide. A majority of the land surrounding the lake is part of the Sierra National Forest, and contains campgrounds, recreation areas and tourist accommodations.

Coarsegold – the first gateway town you'll encounter coming north on Highway 41 from Fresno. It covers the Yosemite Lakes Park community on the west side of the highway to the Chukchansi casino on the east, and north past the village up Deadwood mountain. Coarsegold was previously named Coarse-Gold Gulch and Texas Flat by Texas gold miners in 1849.

Fish Camp – a small village just south of the entrance to Yosemite National Park at 5,000 feet in elevation. It houses tourist accommodations, the Yosemite Mountain Sugar Pine Railroad and Tenaya Lodge.

North Fork – a small town southeast of Bass Lake and 14 miles from Oakhurst. Known for being the exact geographic center of California, it is the origin point of the Sierra Vista Scenic Byway and home of the tribal headquarters of the North Fork Rancheria of Mono Indians of California.

Oakhurst – the largest town near the southern entrance of Yosemite National Park, located on the Fresno River, with its town center at the junction of Highways 41 and 49. Originally called Fresno Flats. Oakhurst contains several named neighborhoods like Goldside on the west side of town and Cedar Valley to the north.

The gateway towns are not official municipalities and therefore rely on the county for public services such as law enforcement, fire control, and area government. The most recent census lists the population as 11,000 full-time residents for Oakhurst, alone. Although numbers vary by source, it's safe to say there are approximately 30,000 residents in all of the gateway towns combined, both seasonal and full-time. To get a complete demographic breakdown of the people who live here, check out the website City-Data.com.

The Oakhurst welcome sign

Many of those who were born and raised here come from families who have resided in the area for generations. Their backgrounds are primarily Caucasian-European or Native American. The non-indigenous (Euro-American) people migrated to the area for lucrative gold mining opportunities in the mid-19th century, known as the Gold Rush Era.

The Indigenous Americans in the area belong mainly to the Yokuts and Mono people. The Yokuts—which literally translates to "people"—consists of 60 separate tribes that include the Picayune Rancheria of Chukchansi, the Dumna/Kechayi, Tachi, and Tule River tribes. The Chukchansi are also known for building the large casino and resort on the southern end of Coarsegold.

The Mono people now live predominantly in the town of North Fork and surrounding area. Indigenous tribes were the first inhabitants of this land, and depending on where you live, you may find arrowheads or native artifacts on your property.

We also have a great number of transplants—residents who have moved here from somewhere else, usually looking for a different, simpler way of life. They have an innate desire to be closer to nature, to be part of a smaller community, or are just seeking a quieter lifestyle. A majority of transplanted residents come from within California, either from larger southern California cities like Los Angeles or San Diego, or the northern Bay Area communities like San Francisco and San Jose. Some come here from outside of California for a job or to be closer to family. Local high school graduates who might have left the area for college or a job opportunity will often move back later for the quality of life or to take care of an aging parent.

You'll soon learn that the more people you meet, the more you'll run into your friends around town. Gone are the days when you can flip off that person who cut you off in traffic, because odds are they're your neighbor or the local coffee shop barista you will see daily. The bottom line is that people seem to behave better in a small town because there isn't as much anonymity as there is in the big city. Everyone is connected to one another, and so your personal reputation is everything. You have to relinquish the big city attitude of

"Who cares what they think? I'll never see them again," because chances are, you will.

Between SierraNewsOnline.com, The Sierra Star newspaper, and Mugshots.com, there's not much you can do without the whole community knowing. You might not have ever met your neighbors in the big city, but your new mountain community neighbors are likely to show up at your door to welcome you. Some might leave food from their gardens on your doorstep, or gift you some freshly-laid eggs. Ultimately, our community takes care of our own and we're loyal.

You'll also notice that there is less racial diversity here in the mountain communities than in the city. Most residents are Caucasian and Native American with a smaller percentage of African-Americans, Asians and Hispanics. As far as politics, the residents in our towns tend to be more conservative, however liberals can easily find pockets of like-minded friends through groups like the Mountain Democrats Club (www.YosemiteDems.com). If you socialize often and join the various service organizations in town, you'll find people of all political persuasions.

Moving from a large metropolitan area—or even the suburbs—can be a big adjustment, but if you are missing the mall, or must see a movie in IMAX, Fresno is only a 45-minute drive. And then at the end of the day, you can return to the mountains and your corner of paradise. Those of us who have made the move from a big city know that mountain life can be an incredible change, but most agree it's a change for the better.

THE CLIMATE

Traveling north on California Highway 41 from Fresno to Oakhurst, you slowly climb in elevation, moving from the grasslands of the San Joaquin Valley to the rounded hills of the oak savannah. As you continue toward Yosemite, the density of oak increases as the occasional Foothill Pine elbows through for its fair share of sun and precipitation. From Coarsegold through Oakhurst and beyond you're in an oak-woodlands zone, where you'll experience some of the most diverse and productive habitats in the world, supporting thousands of plant and animal species. The number of conifer trees increases above 3,000 feet, and as you drive farther north from Oakhurst into Fish Camp, the sugar pine, ponderosa pine, red cedar, Douglas fir and mountain dogwood make up the majority of the forest.

If you've moved from the relatively temperate climate of Southern California, or the rainy and foggy Bay Area, welcome to the land of four easy seasons. The cold isn't too cold, the hot doesn't blister too often, and in between are hundreds of outstanding days and nights to enjoy your natural surroundings—if only from the comfort of your couch in front of a roaring fire.

In fact, once you settle here, the glorious colors of changing leaves in fall, splashy winter sunsets, abundance of flora and fauna in spring, and star-filled summer nights will make you feel at home in all seasons.

AVERAGE TEMPERATURES

Winter temperatures in Oakhurst tend to be in the 30s (degrees Fahrenheit) for the lows, and upper 50s for the highs, depending on your elevation. The reality is the temps can dip into the teens at night and yet it's not uncommon to have winter days with beautiful temperatures in the 60s or even higher. You'll need a good winter jacket, along with the usual hats, scarves, and gloves—and that's just if you intend to inhabit what locals call the "lower country," or that which is below 5,000 feet in elevation.

If you plan to venture into the "high country" above 5,000 feet, you'll also want a good pair of snow boots (helpful hint: buy your new snow boots in spring or summer for the best prices and availability). The higher elevations include many of the more popular sites in Yosemite National Park, where winter temps regularly drop down to the mid-20s and below. In the winter months, the average high temperatures in Yosemite reach about the mid-40s.

Summer temperatures in the foothills will reach the mid-to-upper 90s from May through September, depending on the year, with little to no humidity. It's not uncommon for the temperature to soar over 100 degrees in town, and if it does, that's when you might want to head to the higher elevations for some relief.

The San Joaquin Valley (Fresno, Clovis, Madera) will usually be five to ten degrees hotter than here in the foothills. The change in temperature between day and night is more pronounced up in the mountains, so even if the heat gets to be as high as the 90s during the day, you most likely will enjoy the evening lows, where it could drop back into the 50s. The drastic change from hot to cool gives you a chance to throw open the windows at night to let the soothing breezes in—along with the soundtrack of the season, which includes crickets, cicadas, and frogs.

STARRY SKIES

In any season, one of the first major differences you'll notice in the rural mountain area is that it's very dark outside at night. It may sound like a basic concept and perhaps you've camped here, or stayed with friends, or maybe you grew up on the outskirts of nowhere, and so pitch black night is normal to you. If not, make sure you know where you are at night, what creature may be lurking nearby, and be cautious while driving the country roads. Use all the light you have available to you, from your car's brights to the flashlight on your cell phone.

On the other hand, some nights you'll be astonished by the brightness of the moon or the sheer number of stars will threaten to blow your mind into little curious bits. To use an overused word, it really is *awesome* to witness the mass of stars over the Sierra at night.

Suddenly you may find yourself becoming passionate about the Perseids annual meteor shower, telling your friends back in the city it's one of the brightest in the Northern Hemisphere when it takes place every summer, or you'll learn to call each of the full moons by its native name: Old Moon and Wolf Moon replacing January and February in your lunar vocabulary. One of the reasons people give for moving to the mountains is a strong and persistent desire to become closer with nature, so embrace your wild side and revel in the gifts of the natural world in the Sierra. For more information visit the websites www.TimeandDate.com and www.EarthSky.org.

LOCAL NEWS

Aside from several television news stations in Fresno and the Fresno Bee newspaper, we have a handful of reputable news organizations in the foothills.

Sierra News Online posts events, traffic incidents, fire news often in real time, and have built a strong following on Facebook and their website: SierraNewsOnline.com.

The Sierra Star is a printed newspaper, published weekly on Thursdays for over fifty years. In order to subscribe to the Sierra Star, you must also subscribe to the Fresno Bee. Both papers are owned by The McClatchy Company, the second largest news publisher in the United States. Kiosks for the paper can be found outside all the major grocery stores and at service stations throughout the area.

Java Mountain News is a monthly publication in which you will find a monthly community calendar, public interest articles, ads by local merchants, and nostalgic trivia games. Java Mountain News is distributed to most of the local retail establishments including grocery stores and coffee shops.

WHAT'S IN A NAME?

The town of Oakhurst was originally named Fresno Flats. Charming, right? The name *Fresno* is a Spanish word meaning "ash tree." Old Fresno Flats was a bustling little town, host to the farming, gold mining, and lumber industries. The story goes that in 1885, a stagecoach on its way to Yosemite was held up at gunpoint. Two Fresno Flats residents, Charley Meyers and Willie Prescott, were identified, accused, and arrested for the crime. But after three mistrials, the county gave up trying to convict the men and they were set free.

After that, the town was closely associated with both the crime and the suspects. Fresno Flats became known as "the town where Charley Meyers robbed the stagecoach." Charley's wife Kitty, who served as the town's postmaster, was duly embarrassed by the association and petitioned to change the town's name to Oakhurst. She succeeded, and Fresno Flats became Oakhurst on February 28, 1912.

SPEAKING OF NAMES...

You may have read about the hoopla surrounding the landmark names in Yosemite National Park. According to a concession contract penned long ago with Delaware North Company, DNC was required to purchase the brand names when it began its service to the Park in 1993. Now that the contract has been taken over by a new concessioner, Aramark Corp, DNC required them to purchase the names or relinquish the rights to use them for profit. Aramark chose not to purchase the brand names, and so in early 2016 many of the historic hotels and tourist spots had to rebrand themselves.

Here is a guide to the new names in Yosemite National Park—which, by the way, is another of the pre-owned brand names that cannot be used on any merchandise.

Historic Name	New Name
The Ahwahnee Hotel	Majestic Yosemite Hotel
The Wawona Hotel	Big Trees Lodge
Badger Pass Ski Area	Yosemite Ski & Snowboard Area
Curry Village	Half Dome Village
Yosemite Lodge at the Falls	Yosemite Valley Lodge

MOUNTAIN TIME

The concept of time is interpreted a little differently up here in the foothills. "Mountain Time," as we've dubbed it, can be a blessing or a curse, depending on your perception and situation. Things move a little more slowly here, and we can always spot a city person by their level of frustration in a slow-moving grocery line. If you're used to getting in and out of an establishment quickly, you might be bothered at first that people stop and chat and catch up on each other's lives. Yes, even in the grocery line, gas station, or bank.

The down side of "Mountain Time" is when you've scheduled a service technician, handyman, or contractor and they arrive three hours later than the scheduled appointment. Although we pass off the phrase as a joke, it's not amusing at all when someone takes "Mountain Time" seriously and has made you wait for hours.

That being said, those of us who have settled here soon realize that it's okay to slow down a little. After all, do we really need to rush off or are we just used to moving at city pace? Stop and smell the pine trees. Taking life a little slower can be a pleasant part of living in a rural area, and has been known to be beneficial for your health.

We know you're from
Southern California when...

• You go out without a coat in the winter…because you don't own one.

• You arrive 20 minutes early to every appointment, because you've factored in traffic.

• You think every place is so quaint it would make a great filming location.

• You attempt to go out to dinner after 10 p.m. only to find everything closed.

• You drive a late-model luxury-class vehicle.

• You call the highways *The* 41 or *The* 49 –a purely L.A. thing.

• You drive to Fresno weekly, at first, so you don't get mall withdrawal.

• You cower from the first person who smiles or talks to you in public.

• You keep remarking on how great the air smells.

• You take hundreds of photos of the deer in your yard.

• You constantly brag to your So Cal friends about how much house (and land) you got for the money.

We know you're from the Bay Area when...

- You refer to "The City" and you mean San Francisco when we mean Fresno.
- You bring a sweater to every outdoor event, even in the summer, because you still think it might be chilly.
- You root for the Giants.
- You ask where the gourmet food is.
- You wonder where all the hybrids have gone.
- You can't believe how low the housing prices are, even when the market here is at a record high.
- You're irritated at how slowly the grocery line is moving because the checker and customer are chatting about their kids.
- A trucker gives you a little wave and you hit the gas, perplexed.
- It starts to sprinkle and you put on a parka.
- You buy top-notch gear, including poles and rain poncho, just to "hike" Bridalveil Fall.
- It starts to snow and you cover your car.

CHAPTER 2
What Came Before Us

Follow any direction the wind blows and you'll take a giant step back in time. Many of the sights, interpretive centers, and festivals in the area celebrate the Gold Rush era with its thousands of '49ers who came to California in search of fortune. Some good-sized nuggets were discovered in Coarsegold around 1850, which subsequently attracted many settlers with gold stars in their eyes. T54he early residents raised children, farmed the land, and provided supplies to miners who continued to migrate to the area. If you take a trip up historic Highway 49, you'll be transported to the olden days as you drive the old stage coach route, passing through mining towns that dot the map of the Mother Lode region.

INDIGENOUS PEOPLE

Long before Europeans began to explore this territory, the first people thrived, including Miwok, Mono and Yokuts. Simply looking down at the rock beneath your feet can reveal a telltale sign of native inhabitants: grinding holes abound, and it's easy to picture women pounding acorns into flour—a process so laborious it's left bowl-shaped divots in the granite. Hundreds of years later, these remnants catch rain and serve as watering holes for some of the animals that populate the mountains.

Native American grinding rock
near the Fresno River

The Wassama Roundhouse in Ahwahnee was built in 1860 and rebuilt after it burned, and now survives as one of only three authentic ceremonial roundhouses in California. It is currently cared for by members of the Miwok tribe. Artifacts in its interpretive center and those found in local museums attest to the richly documented history of the indigenous Americans. The name Wassama means "leaves falling" in Miwok.

ANCIENT SEQUOIAS

The area's oldest known area inhabitants are not people at all, but two remarkable groves of ancient giant sequoia trees. Make a point to visit both the Mariposa Grove of Giant Sequoias in Yosemite National Park, and the lesser-known slice of heaven called Nelder Grove, located just outside of Oakhurst. These majestic sequoia trees are a must-see for any traveler or new resident to the area, towering hundreds of feet above the forest floor. Check out the friends of Nelder Grove at www.**neldergrove**.org for more information about visiting.

From the ancient trees to the first people, followed by the explorers, miners and loggers who survived to build communities from the wilderness of these foothills, this part of the west is unique. The Sierra is well-suited as a home for those

> I always knew it was beautiful here, but living here has given us time to explore these hills and I have had my breath taken away more than I knew was possible. – *Carrie D.*

who wish to combine their love of the natural world with lore and history. There's simply no other place like it in the world.

YOSEMITE NATIONAL PARK

Part of the allure of the gateway communities is what's on the other side of the gate, as Yosemite National Park is truly amazing to have in our proverbial backyard. The park was first protected by proclamation of President Abraham Lincoln in 1864 and now includes nearly 1,200 square miles of rugged valleys, heart-stopping vistas, pristine meadows, alpine lakes, churning streams, and spectacular waterfalls.

Carved from the glaciers dating back thousands of years, Yosemite National Park offers unlimited opportunities for recreation.

It's a little misleading to call Yosemite a park, when much of the land is a vast, densely wooded, steeply-pitched and potentially dangerous environment in which a single false step can lead to disaster. Nevertheless, our very own tourist destination is extremely popular. In an average tourist season, Yosemite hosts over a four million visitors a year, who come for the climbing, rafting, birding, camping, hiking, and sightseeing—along with world-class dining and hotel accommodations—that make the location one of the most visited national parks in the country.

GHOSTS AND SPIRITS

As with any community rich in history, there is always repeated lore of ghosts and spirits. Stop any long-time resident, and they'll spin you a ghost tale or experience they've had in any particular local landmark. Our towns are often visited by paranormal investigators, eager to catch a glimpse, feeling, or EVP (electronic voice print) recording of our dearly departed. If you're into the paranormal, you'll want to check out at least one of the many haunted spots in our area.

Once a restaurant and bar, now a thrift store, The Snow Line Depot at the northern tip of Oakhurst has had its fair share of ghost activity. Owners of the current thrift store report that the spirits are fond of a particular sombrero, which seems to change location overnight. Other ghost activity has been reported throughout the Snow Line's days as a restaurant, specifically in the bar area.

The Tri-County Tuberculosis Sanatorium used to stand where Ahwahnee Hills Regional Park is currently located, off of Highway 49 in Ahwahnee. Established in 1918, the

Sanatorium consisted of several buildings, including a residence for the staff, a children's home, and a school. The hospital closed in 1969, and several of the buildings were converted to The Ahwahnee Hills School for Boys which remained active until 1985. The site is fabled to have many spirits in residence who roam Ahwahnee Park to this day. One park ranger says that people have seen the ghost of a little red-haired girl, giggling at them. An old woman in a blue hospital gown with long grey hair seems to walk the park at night around 10:00 p.m.

The Tri-County Tuberculosis Sanatorium
photo courtesy Fresno Flats Museum and Historical Park

Sierra Sky Ranch, established in 1875, was the first working cattle ranch in the Yosemite gateway area. In 1946, the owners converted Sierra Sky to a hotel and resort and catered to dignitaries and Hollywood celebrities including Marilyn Monroe and John Wayne. Current-day guests have reported ghostly footsteps in the hallways, knocks on doors, crashes, children tugging on their clothing, and even a ghostly kiss on the cheek! There has been so much spirit activity at Sierra Sky Ranch, that if you ask politely, the staff might agree to give you a ghost tour of the hotel, pointing out where most of the specters reside. The television show 20/20 did a segment on the resident ghosts at Sierra Sky Ranch and it has been featured on many ghost hunting programs.

Fresno Flats Historical Village and Park is a museum and park that consists of historical buildings, with ongoing spirit activity reported in every corner. The big yellow Laramore-Lyman house is fabled to have the ghosts of Mr. and Mrs. Laramore in residence, who have been heard running up the steps to the third floor when visitors enter their home. Images of children in 19th-century attire have also been spotted in and around schoolhouse, as well as playing around the park. The most famous spirit of Fresno Flats is "Pete," a child of twelve, who tends to materialize to visiting kids in order to play with them. Animal spirits have also been photographed and spotted on the grounds. Laura, the groundskeeper of Fresno Flats, is happy to provide a ghost tour upon request. For more information about the park, visit www.FresnoFlatsMuseum.org.

The community theater company converted the Snow Line Bowling Alley to a theater in 1972, now called The Golden Chain Theatre. Cast members and theatergoers alike have experienced lights turning on and off, cold spots, and other spooky activity.

Several guests of The Yosemite Valley Lodge in the park have reported waking up to a strange dark figure standing over them. No harm is ever done to the guests, and one guest said that the figure disappeared immediately after she screamed for help.

In the famed Majestic Yosemite Hotel (formerly The Ahwahnee), the ghost of the former proprietor, Mary Curry Tresidder, has been seen walking the halls of its sixth floor where she used to have a private suite. Hotel housekeeping staff members have claimed to see a lone rocking chair in motion in the parlor of the fourth floor suite, even though there is no rocking chair in the room. The hotel's historian speculates that it might just be the ghost of John F. Kennedy, who once stayed in the exact suite and requested a rocking chair for his bad back.

There's another hotel in Yosemite that is known to be haunted, the Big Trees Hotel (formerly The Wawona Hotel). Sometime during the 1920s, a small plane crashed outside the hotel, and the pilot was taken to Moore Cottage where he died from his injuries. People have reported seeing a ghost in pilot's uniform walking up and down the stairs of Moore Cottage. Other guests have reported seeing a rug levitate off the floor in the same guest suite. A chef in the Wawona Hotel's kitchen once reported that a fire alarm that he was standing right next to was allegedly pulled…by no one.

Stories of specters have not kept away the millions of visitors who come to stay at these establishments year after year. In fact, having a ghost-in-residence only enhances a hotel's historical reputation.

CHAPTER 3
Your Mountain Home

Perhaps you're an avid Yosemite fan, and after your third or fourth trip you start thinking about how ideal your life would be if you could achieve your dream of living in the mountains. You imagine the clean air, the quiet nights, and having hundreds of hiking trails just minutes away. Well, many of us have made that dream a reality and you can too. First and foremost, you have to do your research. So congratulations! Just by reading this book you've taken the first step.

The next step is to browse. Even from your home in the big city, you can set aside a couple of hours to browse homes for sale via real estate websites. Depending on what area you desire to live, the zip codes you'll want to search are: 93644 (Oakhurst), 93614 (Coarsegold), 93601 (Ahwahnee), 93604 (Bass Lake), 93643 (North Fork), and 93623 (Fish Camp). Some websites allow you to plot the homes on a map, so you can move the map around to see the exact locations of the homes for sale.

Make a list of your real estate needs—how much you can afford, the number of bedrooms and baths you want, and whether you want one story or two. There are additional things you should consider when moving to this area that you might not have encountered while living in the city.

> "This area is actually one of the more affordable areas in California. We moved here from the Central Coast where it's too expensive to retire!" –*Barbara L.*

How much land are you able to maintain? Do you want to be more secluded or have neighbors close by, and do you want to be part of a homeowner's association like Yosemite Lakes Park with dues and CC&Rs? Do you want to be near a golf course, lake or hiking trail? Do you want a log cabin or a more modern home with drywall? Decide whether you'll need extra acreage for raising livestock or keeping horses. You'll also want to consider how far you're willing to live from the town shopping centers. If you need your coffee shop latté each morning, you may not want to drive 25 minutes to get it. If you have children, you'll want to see how close the home is to the various schools, or you may decide to homeschool. These are all things you can work out before contacting an agent.

If you love water sports, fishing, or own a boat, you might want to gravitate toward the Bass Lake area. If you enjoy hiking, camping or climbing, you might want to seek homes closer to Yosemite National Park. If you love snow sports like snowboarding or skiing, you could look at properties close to or above the snow line, which is currently at around 3,300 feet.

Once you have a list of homes you'd like to see, contact a real estate agent who is local to the mountain area. Having a buyer's agent—at no cost to you—has many advantages when seeking real estate out of town. The most important advantage being that the agent will know the community, neighborhoods, schools, and insurance regulations. Your agent will be your primary conduit and information source to living in the mountain area (other than this book). We do recommend that you hire an agent from within the mountain communities, as those outside of the area—even as close as Fresno—may not have the intimate experience with the area or the local information that you will need throughout your search.

The time you spend looking for homes will depend on how far you've come to do so. If you are flying cross-country, you may just want to set aside a week. If you are driving three to four hours from Southern California or the Bay Area, you may want to do it in several weekends. Make sure your coordinate the trip with your agent, so he or she can be prepared and plan your tour.

On your real estate hunting trips, plan to take in more than the homes you visit. Pay attention to the layout of the towns, the various neighborhoods, shopping and grocery stores, and the weather. Stay in a local hotel. Eat out at our various restaurants and get a feel for the community, the people, and the shops. Talk to us! Many residents are happy to give information about why we love living here.

When you get to the escrow stage, there may be a few differences in the inspection process compared with what you may have experienced in the city or suburbs. If the home has a well for water, for example, you'll want a well inspection and a water test. In addition to a general home inspection you may want to order septic inspection, a survey of the property lines, and pest control checkup. The drought has affected many of the trees in the area, which have been infested with bark beetles, prompting some homebuyers to hire arborists for a tree inspection of the property.

Communicate with your agent over email and inquire about properties you find online. Local agents may know (or can find out) the quirks of a particular home, or if it's currently in contract. According to the local agents, the average "buy cycle" is six months, but it can be more depending on where you're currently located and if you need to sell your existing home.

THINGS TO CONSIDER WHEN VIEWING HOMES

✓ Is the driveway steep? Check to see if you'll be able to get in and out when it's snowy or icy.

✓ Do you need a fenced in yard for your dogs or animals? (See Chapter 10 about pets).

✓ Are you willing to renovate or do construction on a home that may need repair? If you want a bargain, you'll definitely be able to find homes in the area that have not been maintained or redecorated since the last century.

✓ Consider the land acreage and the equipment (or help) you'll need to maintain it.

✓ Is the majority of the property land usable or is it on a steep slope?

✓ Map the closest fire house to the property. You also might want to call the phone company and see how close the property is to a main box.

✓ If the house is powered by propane, check to see if the propane tank was purchased outright or rented. See upcoming section on propane.

YOUR MOVE TO THE MOUNTAINS

If you have the flexibility to do so, try to time your actual move in the spring or fall months. Moving in the heat of summer could be grueling. Our winters can be rainy or icy, depending on the month. March to May or October to November would probably be the ideal time. Avoid big holiday weekends like Memorial Day or Labor Day, as Yosemite draws double and triple the amount of tourists during those times. Tour buses and tourist automobiles and campers can crowd the main roads into the area.

Once you're moved and unpacked, you may get a visitor or two at your front door. Neighbors will want to introduce themselves and meet you. If you go a couple of days without seeing your neighbors, go knock on their doors and introduce yourself! We're a friendly bunch and most will be happy that you did so. Neighbors are also a good source of information about the area. They can answer your questions like, when is trash day, and when do we put out the recycling bin?

One of the most appealing aspects of moving to a rural area is the act of leaving the masses behind. Here you can live large—*really* large—where you have space to stretch out. For some, this means owning a property that's ten or more times larger than any previous home, with land in all directions. One family noted that their chicken run here on their mountain property is equivalent to their entire backyard in the city.

NO TRESPASSING

While property lines should be clearly marked when homes are bought and sold, these lines can become blurred when it comes to pets or even children. Many properties are unfenced, and that means that sometimes other people's animals can find their way into your backyard, and it's equally possible that your precious pet will stray onto your neighbor's property. It's critical that your dogs and cats are micro-chipped in case they wander off beyond your boundary.

It's worth noting that human trespassing upon another person's property is frowned upon in our rural area, but even if you post a clear "No Trespassing" sign, you may still get an unwelcome visitor or two. You'll come to easily recognize people and vehicles that don't belong in your neighborhood, and it's common for residents to share information, including license numbers and descriptions of unrecognized vehicles. Some homeowners have installed home security, including electronic gates and fencing, as well as increasingly common surveillance cameras and devices that let you see and speak to visitors from your cell phone. And then there's the analog security pooch, who may or may not be too friendly. Just be cognizant of your property lines and you should remain safe within your community.

WELL, WELL

Utilities are different in the mountains, starting usually with where and how you get your water. In the city, you pay your water bill on a monthly basis and generally turn on the faucet and water comes out. In the mountains, you may have a neighborhood water utility or you may have a well. It's wise to know the difference.

Across the Sierra tens of thousands of people rely on underground sources for their home's water supply. Ground water primarily occurs in fractures in the hard rock. When you purchase a home with a well, you will be required to have a well inspection that will measure the depth of the well and GPM (gallons per minute) at which the well draws water. The deepest wells are generally about 1500 feet, while many are finding water 800 to 900 hundred feet deep and occasionally at more shallow depths.

Some homeowners share a well with a neighbor. If this is the case, you will want to have a special well agreement drafted and signed to go along with your other home purchase documents. The well agreement should include clear instructions on who will cover expenses in the event of mechanical failure or extreme drought resulting in no water. In the last several years, the diminishing supply of groundwater has made wells work harder, causing many homeowners to fork over thousands of dollars to have their wells refurbished with new pipe, wire, or motors. Some have even run out of water, required a new well to be drilled, a very daunting and expensive process.

WATER CONDITIONING

If the home you're in doesn't already have a water conditioning system, you may want to have your water tested to see if it's corrosive due to mineral content. If so, it could eat through your pipes or water heater, or build up on appliances like washing machine or dishwasher, causing major damage that could cost from hundreds to tens of thousands of dollars.

An easy test to see if you have "soft" or corrosive water is if you see colored rings in your toilet bowl and/or ceramic sink. By the way, those rings can be easily removed with a plain pumice stone from the dollar store!

Be aware that if you do have a water conditioning system, you will probably get the opposite—hard water residue—on your dishes. There are dishwasher additives for hard water, an easy fix available at most grocery stores.

WOOD STOVES AND OTHER HEAT SOURCES

One of life's little pleasures in the mountains is having a fireplace or wood stove and actually needing to use it. With nighttime temperatures that stay chilly for many months of the year, you will want to know where to purchase your wood, how much to pay for it, and how to build a good fire without a lot of fuss.

Homes may come with a wood burning fireplace, wood stove, pellet stove, electric or gas fireplace, forced air heating, solar heating or some combination of any or all of these luxuries. Wood burning stoves and fireplaces are legal for use depending on elevation, and whether or not your property has access to natural gas (propane is not considered a natural gas.) In some cases, homeowners may be eligible for grants of up to $1,000 to switch out an old, inefficient wood stove for a new, clean-burning model.

As far as buying wood, ask your neighbors for recommendations for a reputable wood seller, and when you find one, stick with him or her. A cord of seasoned oak firewood should sell for anywhere between $175 to $225, delivered, and in some cases, stacked. A full cord measures 4' x 4' x 8'.

Being located close to the farmland and orchards of the San Joaquin Valley has its advantages. You can purchase almond wood, for instance, to mix in with your base of oak. Pine firewood is nice, as long as it's not bull pine, also known as Foothill Pine. The wood of this particular tree leaves behind a tarry residue that makes it undesirable for burning.

Not only is this tarry residue messy when it comes to cleaning out your stove, it also sticks to the inside of your chimney, where buildup of creosote can cause a potentially devastating chimney fire if left uncleaned. If you haven't heard the term "chimney sweep" since the last time you watched Mary Poppins, now is the time to get used to it again. A qualified chimney sweep is an important part of mountain home care and safety. Once again, check your phone book and consider having your chimney inspected and cleaned at least once a year.

You may need more than a single cord of wood each year, depending on use and weather, so stay one step ahead of the game and purchase your firewood in the summer when it's not so sought-after. Store your firewood away from the home during summer according to fire wise recommendations so it doesn't become a hazard. Some would argue the very best wood is the wood you gather on your property, cut with your own chainsaw, and burn in your own home while you relax, fireside, with a light aperitif and a satisfied smile.

With all the dead trees being cut down in the area, many people are offering firewood free of charge if you haul it and split it yourself. This can be a huge cost-savings during the winter months, so stay connected with the community online and put a call out "In search of wood, will pick up!" on various social networks.

GAS/PROPANE

Back in the city, many people have a gas company, and if the bill was paid the gas stayed on. Here in the foothills, the gas is propane, and it's delivered in giant trucks and pumped into tanks on individual properties.

The average mountain home comes with a 250 gallon propane tank that's either rented from a local company or purchased outright, where you have the choice of companies from which you order. The rental cost of a tank is under $100 yearly, whereas the propane gas itself is priced per gallon and fluctuates like automobile gas. As with wood, it's best to purchase a full tank of propane in the summer when prices are typically lower.

Each propane tank comes with a gauge so you know what percentage remains full; when it gets down to about 15% you should give your propane company a call to request a refill.

Some companies do "make rounds" of their regular customers and will refill your tank automatically when you get under 50%. Make sure you indicate to your propane company whether you want to order "will call" or have them determine your fill rate. If you do decide on will call, check your tank level regularly so you don't run out.

You should also know where and how to turn the valve on your propane tank off in case of an emergency, such as a wildfire evacuation.

SOLAR AND ELECTRIC

While some foothill homeowners have installed passive solar power to cut down on the cost and use of electricity, many homes are still serviced by Pacific Gas & Electric (PG&E). Throughout the foothills, you'll notice PG&E maintaining the lines, trimming and removing hazardous trees, and cleaning up after storms. PG&E will sometimes want access to their meters on your property, and in many cases will drive up your road to make sure their power poles are unimpeded by poison oak and other foliage, for which they'll spray.

The electric company will also inspect powerlines on your property on a regular basis, and trim or remove dead trees that constitute a hazard.

PHONE, INTERNET, AND TELEVISION

Choices for landline telephone and internet are limited to just a couple of companies in the foothills: Sierra Telephone, Ponderosa, and Northland Communications. For cell phones, some people say Verizon is the better choice while others swear by AT&T. Cell service will be spotty in places, no matter what carrier you choose. Options for television service include but are not limited to Northland Cable Television, Sierra Tel television service, Dish Network and

Direct TV. For "cable cutters"—those who have bravely canceled their cable or satellite TV—there's always streaming services for Smart TVs and plug-in devices such as AppleTV, Roku, or Amazon Fire, that enable viewers to stream just about any network for a price.

A word about the phone book: in larger cities these have gone by the way of fax machines and pagers. But here in a small community, they're still very valuable. Whether you're new to the area or a permanent resident, make sure to pick one up at Sierra Telephone or the Sierra Tel Business Center. Many local businesses still strongly believe in the printed page and you'll find more of them listed in the phonebook than have websites online. It also includes local emergency numbers, service organizations, and a wide variety of information you can't find anywhere else. And of course, all phone books are free.

TRASH, RECYCLING AND THE TRANSFER STATION

Most foothill residents pay a nominal quarterly fee to have their trash picked up at the curb by Emadco Disposal Services. Emadco (short for Eastern Madera County) also provides a recycling program, and will provide separate containers to you with your service. Be advised that Emadco still picks up on most major holidays.

For larger items or those who do not want to pay for curbside pickup, you can take your refuse to the North Fork transfer station at 33699 Malum Ridge Road. Often called "The Dump" it is actually not a landfill, but a facility that will transfer your trash to big trucks and haul it far, far away.

There are also several privately-owned recycling companies that will collect and recycle everything from electronics to hazardous waste. Both Yosemite High School and Minarets High School have free county-sponsored hazardous waste disposal days, so watch for them on your local calendar.

If you're in the mood for a massive cleaning or in the middle of a remodel project, Emadco also offers affordable dumpster rental, which they will deliver and pick up at your convenience.

CLEARING AND FIRE SAFETY

It's easier to live successfully with nature when you learn to strike a balance between "letting it be" and fire risk management. In the Yosemite mountain towns we are required to clear the fire hazards for at least 100 feet around our houses, a process known as *hazard fuel reduction*. In other words, prepare to get very friendly with a weed-whacker, or get the name of someone reliable who can help. The objective is to create defensible space around your home, which requires cutting grass short and trimming trees so that nothing hangs down low. Piles of dried brush are either chipped into pieces that will degrade efficiently, mulched, recycled or slowly burned according to the required Burn Permit.

Open burning in the mountain area is only allowed on specified burn days, and as long as the homeowner has a valid burn permit. Burn permits are free and available through your local fire station or the forestry office. You may burn natural vegetation for maintaining fire breaks around buildings, and the materials to be burned must originate from the property on which it is burned. Waste burning is prohibited in all areas of Madera County.

To find out if burning is allowed on any given day, call: (877) 429-2876. Burn days are determined by a number of meteorological conditions, including characteristics that would enable smoke to adequately disperse. Having said that, remember that just because you *can* burn doesn't mean you *should* burn. The news is full of stories about escaped burn piles. Common sense applies, and if it's hot, dry, windy or you lack experience, proceed with caution or not at all. For more information on hazard fuel burning and allowed burn days as designated by the San Joaquin Valley Air Pollution Control District, contact the District at www.valleyair.org.

Coarsegold resident chips wood for fuel reduction

SUMMER AND WILDFIRES

Along with the rise in temperature, summer also brings an increase in wildfires, endangering our landscape and homes. Over the last several years, our drought-stricken, beetle-infested pine trees have suffered a major die-off in the Sierra National Forest and surrounding areas. Despite the one-two knock-out combination of water shortage and pestilence, the forest is constantly renewing itself and the mostly-coniferous woodland we see today may give way to a more open and rocky savannah in the distant future. In the meantime, be on alert.

MC ALERT EMERGENCY NOTIFICATION

If you live in or travel through Madera County, you'll want to sign up for MC Alert, a free service that enables you to be contacted with critical warnings in case of emergencies. To register, go to www.mcalert.org. The database already contains landline numbers, but if you want to add cell phone, work phone, email, or fax, you must input those additional numbers through which you'd like to be notified. All information is kept confidential.

Once you've registered your notification numbers, the MC Alert system will text and/or call you in the event of a pre-evacuation, an actual fire evacuation, or a threat to your health or safety—according to the contact preferences you entered. If you do not acknowledge receipt of the message, the system will continue to try to contact you until you confirm that you have been reached.

CALL 911 TO REPORT A FIRE

According to the California Wildland Firefighting Group, more than 90% of wildfires are caused by people. In recent history, the causes of these fires have been attributed to kids playing, vehicular malfunction, and what many would call the plain stupidity of burning an animal carcass in the middle of the dry, summer woods. Still, each of these causes comes down to a person, not an act of nature. While summer storms in the Sierra often generate lightning, the resulting fires are usually in the wilderness and can naturally burn themselves out over time. One of the most common causes of wildfire is an unattended campfire or one that's been inefficiently extinguished.

California residents and visitors alike know that some wildfires do not go out quickly, and even if your home isn't directly threatened by flames it's still possible your health could be at risk. Fires that burn for weeks and even months release particulate into the air that can travel for miles. Consult your doctor if you have a breathing condition that may require you to wear a mask during wildfire season.

For more information on how you can prevent wildfires, check out One Less Spark, One Less Wildfire: www.preventwildfireca.org/OneLessSpark.

CHAPTER 4
The Social Scene

You'll rarely see Bentleys cruising Highway 41, fancy furs in church, or any competition for luxury. If this is something that is important to you, you'll have to adjust your expectations. Just like Paris Hilton in the reality show, this is truly "The Simple Life." Although we do have a lot of fun things to do, they won't require you to get the diamonds out of the safe.

DATING IN THE MOUNTAINS

According to City-Data's statistics, over 35% of our mountain residents are single: either never married, divorced, or widowed. That sounds like this would be a lush dating pool, but courting in the mountains is a bit different than in the big cities.

Because our community is so small and "everyone knows everyone" there really is not much anonymity in the dating process. One single female homeowner posted a profile on a popular dating website and received an online "wink" from her gardener. *Awkward!*

The dating sites are helpful as a starting point to know who around town is single and who is looking. After perusing the sites, though, you should do your own research. How long has this person lived in the mountains? Does he or she have an ex in town? Ask friends and neighbors about your potential date's personal and professional reputations.

If you are willing to widen your search to Fresno, Clovis, Madera, and cities that are a little further out, you'll get a larger dating pool. Of course, that means either you or your date will have to make a significant drive to be together. It's up to you and your lifestyle on which "pool" you prefer.

If you do decide to date within the community, take heed: 1. everyone will know, 2. he or she may be an ex of a friend, and 3. if it doesn't work out, you still have to live in the same small community with them. To that respect, it's always a good idea to remain friendly, when you can.

OUR COMMUNITY ONLINE

The Yosemite gateway residents are very active online, as well. There are many local Facebook groups that you can join as a resident, or even if you are planning a move to the area:

Mountain Area Auto Sales and Swap – Autos and parts for sale

Mountain Area Chicken Chicks – All about raising poultry

Mountain Classic Cars – Antique auto enthusiasts, discussion and sales

Mountain Dog Watch – Lost and found dog listings

Mountain Fire and Emergency – Fire and accident info

Mountain Garden and Farm Swap – Items for sale

Mountain Jobs – Job listings and In Search Of

Mountain Men's Swap – Items for sale (not for swapping men!)

Mountain Swap – Items for sale, like a local Craigslist

Mountain Swap II – The Business Page – Place to ask for business referrals or promote your business

Mountain Talk – General information and discussion

Mountain Writers – Writing resources and discussion

Oakhurst Area – General information and discussion

Yosemite Area – General information and discussion

Yosemite Area Homes for Sale – Real estate listings

Yosemite Dog Enthusiasts – Canine Talk and Photos

Yosemite History – Discussion and photos of our area's past

Yosemite Kids – Discussion on parenting and schools

Yosemite Marketplace – Items for sale and business listings

Yosemite Treasures – Antiques & Collectibles

Yosemite Western Artists – Discussion on art and artists

COMMUNITY RESOURCES

Whether you're thinking of moving to the mountains or already live here, you'll want to stop in and see the helpful staff and volunteers at the Visit Yosemite|Madera County visitors bureau in Oakhurst. At the visitors bureau you'll find maps, brochures, displays, and people who are willing and able to answer your questions about the area and its many activities and amenities. Before you even get to the visitors bureau, take a look at their website YosemiteThisYear.com, where you'll find well-organized and informative pages with links to a downloadable visitor's guide and a visitor's app for smartphones.

Each of the larger neighboring towns has at least one organization dedicated to business development and community activities, with Chambers of Commerce in Oakhurst, Bass Lake, North Fork, and Coarsegold. The chambers rely mainly on volunteers from the business community and frequently partner with area attractions to host community events. The Bass Lake Chamber helps put on the big Fourth of July fireworks display from a barge in the water, the Coarsegold Chamber sponsors several events in the historic village, and the North Fork Boosters are responsible for the Loggers Jamboree. These annual events are just a few examples—see Chapter 6 for more information on how the Chambers can help your business.

> "We moved here in 1999. I love the way everyone comes together to help each other. If you know of a true need here, you jump in to help if you can…we all take care of each other." – *Liz L.*

SERVICE ORGANIZATIONS

You may have noticed a scenic overlook with a large sign welcoming visitors to Oakhurst about halfway over Deadwood mountain between Oakhurst and Coarsegold. Bordering that sign are the logos and emblems for the multitude of service organizations that support the local community and frequently participate in outreach beyond the foothills to other regions, states and countries around the globe. Our community non-profit organizations help to improve the lives of our community residents. These organizations include, and are not limited to, the following:

Ahwahnee Hills Community Council
www.ahwahneepark.org

Bass Lake Education Foundation
www.basslakeedfund.org

Caring Veterans of America
bit.ly/caringveterans

Central California Animal Disaster Team (CCADT)
www.ccadt.org

Eastern Madera County SPCA
www.emcspca.org

Fresno Flats Historical Village & Park
www.fresnoflatsmuseum.org

Friends of Nelder Grove
www.neldergrove.org

Friends of YOSAR (Yosemite Search and Rescue)
www.friendsofyosar.org

Friends of the Oakhurst Branch Library (FOBL)
www.oakhurstfobl.com

H.O.W. - Helping One Woman
www.facebook.com/HOWoakhurst

La Sierra Guild (Children's Hospital)
www.lasierraguild.org

Mountain Community Women
www.mountaincommunitywomen.com

North Fork Women's Club

Oakhurst Community Center
www.oakhurstcommunitycenter.com

Oakhurst Elks Lodge
www.oakhurstelks.com

Oakhurst Sierra Rotary
www.oakhurstrotary.org

Oakhurst Sierra Sunrise Rotary
www.oakhurstsierrasunriserotary.org

Sierra Lions Club
www.sierralionsclub.org

Sierra Mountain Little League
www.sierramountainll.org858tt05554e

Sierra Oakhurst Kiwanis
www.oakhurstkiwanis.org

Sierra Senior Society
bit.ly/sierraseniors

Soroptimist International of the Sierras
www.soroptimistofthesierras.org

Vision Academy of the Arts
www.visionacademyofthearts.org

Wild Wonderful Women
www.wwwoakhurst.org

Yosemite Conservancy
www.yosemite.org

FAITH & WORSHIP

People of most faiths will have no trouble finding a church in which to practice their chosen religions, keeping in mind that the closest Temple or Mosque to the foothills is located more than 40 miles away in the Central Valley. Followers of other flocks may check the Sierra Tel Yellow Pages for a complete listing of over 30 churches in the area.

The Positive Living Center in Oakhurst holds non-denominational services each Sunday for those who wish to come together in prayer and spiritual meditation. They also hold healing services and offer workshops on a variety of subjects in the fields of personal growth and spirituality.

WHAT'S WITH ALL THE CLASSIC CARS?

You may have noticed driving through town that there are an extraordinary number of vintage automobiles in the area. From early Model A Fords to fab 50's Fairlanes, you will eventually catch a sweet classic cruising the mountain roads on a hot summer night. So where did all the classic cars come from and why are they all here?

Skip Bradlee's trophy-winning classics

The classic car craze all started with the CamTwisters in Fresno, a fifty-year-old car club that is still in existence today. Then in 1997, the Mountain Road Rattlers formed up here in the mountain communities. The Road Rattlers originally only allowed pre-World War II vehicles from the 1920's and 30's, but now accepts all classic car enthusiasts.

They say collecting classic cars is like a disease, once you catch it, it's hard to cure. For older folks, it brings back fond memories of their youth. For those who are retired, it gives them something to work on. For younger drivers, it's a way to own a unique vehicle and connect with the past.

Classic car collecting has caught on in the mountain area towns, and whether you're an enthusiast, an owner, or just a fan, there are a multitude of car shows and cruise nights throughout the good-weather months where you admire the cars and talk to the owners about their restorations.

To take a gander at many fine autos together in one spot, visit one of our many car shows throughout the summer:

Miller's Landing Car Show – Bass Lake, May

Coarsegold Veterans Car Show – Coarsegold Historic Village, July

North Fork "Hot August Night" Car Show – Downtown North Fork, August

Kiwanis Run for the Gold Car Show – Oakhurst Park, September

Fall Festival Classic Car Exhibition – Oakhurst Park, October

Mariposa Yosemite Hot Rod & Custom Car Show – Mariposa Fairgrounds, October

CHAPTER 5
All the Happenings

You may think that moving to the mountains means you're isolating yourself from the "real world" and that there will be nothing to do. That couldn't be further from the truth. There are many unique and interesting things to do in the Yosemite mountain towns in all seasons, including some that you might not find anywhere else. In good weather, there is an event or festival or parade almost every weekend, so it's important to check the community calendars on a regular basis.

WHAT DO YOU DO FOR FUN?

Shopping is definitely an activity here in the foothills, and though you won't find a mall or big-box store, our area boasts many charming shops where you can find almost everything.

Our mountain towns also put on numerous events and festivals, happening throughout the year. In certain months you can't go anywhere without running into a peddler's fair, craft show, food and wine festival, pizza-judging contest, rib or shrimp or crab fest, or some other event that is welcome fun for tourists and locals, alike.

Area service organizations frequently contribute to the overall good of the community with their charitable acts, and also sponsor fun events throughout the four seasons.

Do you like art? The number and quality of artists here is unparalleled, which means there's always an opening or a reception to attend. Oakhurst even has its own Gallery Row, and the annual Sierra Art Trails open studio tour in early fall. Interested in learning about everything from Audubon to taxes and all that's in between? The local libraries offer presentations and workshops nearly every weekend.

In the center of Oakhurst, we have the six-screen Met Cinema movie theater. If you like live theater, you can head up the 41 to the Golden Chain Theatre, a company of talent that produces stage shows all year long. In North Fork, check out the productions of Squirrel Cage Theatre.

The mountain towns are also home or stomping grounds to some of the best musicians around. Choirs and choral groups abound and are especially noticeable at the holidays.

> "I moved here ten years ago from Sacramento. The biggest surprise was all of the mountain community events. It's something I've always wanted for my family. –Melissa C.

Artists frequently showcase at local venues and festivals, and several establishments feature live music and/or open mic nights. Be sure to check out the well-received Coolwater Ranch house concerts in Nipinnawasse, where globally recognized musicians perform in an intimate, unplugged style in the living room of a horse ranch.

If you're interested in becoming part of a sports team you can join the community swimmers who work out at the Baker Swim Complex at Yosemite High School or join a local team for adult soccer. A handful of local gyms and wellness centers offer everything from aerobics to yoga, with some spin, Pilates, and even belly dancing on the side.

The community centers in each town are little hotbeds of entertainment where you'll find some of the most serious fun at competitive bingo and other events designed to get neighbors meeting neighbors.

If you want to learn horseback riding or already know how to ride, we have an active equestrian community. The Sierra Freepackers are an organized group of riders who've formed a nonprofit club devoted to cleaning up hiking and riding trails in cooperation with Sierra National Forest officials. If bucking broncos or barrel racing are more your thing, the newly PRCA-sanctioned rodeo grounds in Coarsegold are a hub for horses and their people, too. Yosemite Lakes Park has its own equestrian center for the convenience of the horse crowd.

The area is populated by citizens who love their pets, so it's common to meet up with friends and pups for a wagging walk 'n talk along dog-friendly trails. There's scenic walking, hiking and biking on the back roads, around the lake, or on trails through the mountains, and plenty of races, marathons, and triathlons. Bass Lake and other recreation areas offer practically unlimited ways to have fun on and off the water, swimming, paddling, kayaking, fishing, rafting, water-skiing, boating and just hanging out.

To many a transplant's surprise, there is always *something* going on in the Yosemite mountain towns. We've curated the following list of events and activities that take place in our area throughout the year.

SPRING

Farmers Markets – Almost every community hosts an open-air farmers market during the better weather months, May through October. The farmers markets draw gardeners, crafters, artisans, and farmers from all over the area with goods including fresh organic eggs, produce, homemade oil and vinegar, and bakery treats. Start with the market closest to you but be sure to check out the rest, too. You'll find different vendors at each market. The following are the current farmers markets as of this writing, but check before you go as dates/times can change: *Oakhurst*: True Value parking lot, 40596 Westlake Dr., Thursdays 4:00 p.m. *Coarsegold*: Coarsegold Historic Village, 35300 CA-41, Fridays 2:00-7:00 p.m. and Sundays at 11:00 a.m. *Bass Lake:* Pines Village, Bass Lake, Wednesdays 3:00 p.m.

Elegant Auction – The Elegant Auction takes place each spring and is the sole benefit to support the nonprofit, privately-owned Oakhurst Community Park. The Elegant Auction committee holds a silent auction, rousing live auction, music, full dinner buffet, complimentary champagne and dessert bar. It's a nice evening to dress up and donate to a worthy, local, community cause.

Coarsegold Rodeo – An annual event that takes place in the first weekend of May in Coarsegold. The rodeo includes vendors, exhibits, family events, food, dance, barrel racing, and pro rodeo excitement for all ages. Coarsegold Rodeo Grounds, 44777 Rodeo Grounds, Coarsegold. For more information, visit www.coarsegoldrodeo.com.

Antique & Classic Wooden Boat Show – The Pines Resort hosts an antique and classic boat show, which usually coincides with the Miller's Landing Classic Car Show.

Bass Lake Fishing Derby – Fishing competition in May that offers a total purse of over $50,000, with fish tagged for as much as $10,000 each.

Honorary Mayor Events – **Each year** Oakhurst holds an Honorary Mayoral Election where individual candidates run to benefit a local charity. It includes ten weeks of charitable fundraising events and entertainment, and ends with the Honorable Mayor title going to the candidate who raised the most money.

Raymond Parade & Family Fun Day – The charming old town of Raymond, located just west of Coarsegold and Yosemite Lakes Park, sponsors a fun day for family including a parade, crafts, swap meet, food, raffle and arts. Raymond is located up Highway 415 near Coarsegold.

German Fest – In March, the Oakhurst Chamber of Commerce sponsors a full four-course German-style dinner (think Bratwurst, Deutsches Brot, Apfelstrudel) with raffle, live auction, and music.

Woodcarvers' Rendezvous – Taking place over a full week, the Woodcarvers' Rendezvous offers classes, camaraderie, and fun sponsored by the Yosemite Visitors' Bureau and the California Carvers Guild. It hosts carving sessions, demonstrations and seminars for all levels of carvers. Service organizations pitch in to sponsor dinners, a pancake breakfast, and other events during the week.

Relay For Life – Eastern Madera County is known for its amazing support of Relay for Life organized by the American Cancer Society. Groups, individuals, schools, clubs, service organizations and businesses band together for 24 hours of fundraising, continuously walking the high school track in Oakhurst, remembering those who've been lost to cancer and celebrating survivors. Tens of thousands of dollars are raised every year for the cause.

Oakminster Dog Show – Organized as a benefit for the Eastern Madera County SPCA, the Oakminster Dog Show is an inclusive event that's run much like its famous Westminster counterpart, but with regular family dogs invited to participate in a large number of categories, including mutts of all sorts. Great for families and any friendly dogs, with prizes and ribbons and all proceeds to benefit the EMC SPCA no-kill shelter fund.

Sock Hop – The local Elks Lodge sponsors an annual 50s Sock Hop with dancing to music from the mid-century, a happy hour and full dinner. Oakhurst Elks Lodge #2724, 42844 Highway 41, Oakhurst.

SUMMER

Coarsegold Peddlers' Fair – On Memorial Day and Labor Day weekends, the Coarsegold Historic Village hosts a Peddlers Fair on the green with all kinds of antiques, collectibles, crafts, and food vendors.

Classic Car Shows/Cruise Night – Many residents in the mountain area share a passion for antique and vintage automobiles. From spring to fall, there seems to be a classic car show almost every month. Whether you're a collector or just a fan, these shows are loads of fun with food, raffles, activities, a generous number of categories, and trophies for the winning cars.

Loggers Jamboree – Yes, our little community has a historic jamboree! Organized by the North Fork Boosters, this event pays tribute to the loggers of the past when North Fork was a mill town, and those keeping the tradition alive today. With hot saw and axe throwing competitions, food, games, a ball, parade, and even the crowning of a Jamboree Queen, this event is a fun way to spend a summer weekend and enjoy the rich history of the area.

Live Music – Several of the local establishments host live music in the summer evenings. Pizza Factory has live jazz on Thursdays, and Queen's Inn/Idle Hour Winery hosts live music on selected weekends. South Gate Brewery and Ducey's on the Lake also host periodic live music events. Check the community calendar for exact dates and times.

Sounds of Solstice - The mountain community music festival that takes place in the beginning of summer in the Oakhurst Community Park and benefits the Boys and Girls Club. For more information visit SoundsofSolstice.com

Bass Lake – There are many activities in and around the lake for families, couples, and singles, alike. Many of the resorts provide fishing boat, party boat, or paddle boat rentals by the hour, half day or full day. If you like water sports, you can rent a canoe, kayak or jet ski for fun on the lake. There are several campgrounds and picnic areas for the day visitor or those who want to stay longer.

Bass Lake also hosts a Fourth of July Boat Parade and fireworks show. In a combined effort by the Bass Lake Chamber, The Pines, Bass Lake Water Sports, and Miller's Landing, the lake lights up with the sights and sounds of Independence Day. All day long area merchants celebrate with special festivities for families and a colorful boat show.

Sierra Mono Museum Pow Wow & Indian Fair Days –
Usually taking place the first weekend of August, the Pow
Wow is an authentic Native American gathering that
includes music, dance, food, crafts, and competitions
celebrating native heritage and culture. Although it began
in North Fork, the pow wow is currently held at Minarets
High School in O'Neals. For more information visit:
SierraMonoMuseum.org/powwow.

FALL

Heritage Parade and Mountaineer Days – A festival put on
to benefit Oakhurst's Fresno Flats Historic Park and to
celebrate the founding of the town. This weekend event
includes games, food, vendors, and even an old-fashioned
town parade with fire trucks, mounted rangers, marching
bands, vintage cars and more!

Heritage Days Parade

Authors Faire – You won't believe how many authors live in the mountain towns until you visit the Oakhurst Branch Library Author's Faire. Each fall dozens of local authors gather to sign and sell their books and answer questions about writing, storytelling, and publishing.

Lutz Apple Farm - The foothills were once home to numerous apple farms, and now, at least one remains. For a short time in the fall, usually a few weeks in September or October depending on the harvest, the Lutz family Apple Farm opens to the public on Road 426 in Oakhurst. Not only can people pick their own bushel of apples in a multitude of varieties, but they also offer fresh apple cider, made daily.

Animal Faire – Sponsored by the Eastern Madera County SPCA, the show is open to dogs, cats, chickens, pigs, lizards and you-name it, allowing residents to show off their pets in many different fun competitions and includes a traditional blessing of the animals.

Sierra Art Trails – The first weekend each October, local artists open their homes and studios for Sierra Art Trails. With the purchase of an Art Trails catalog, two guests have access to bios and maps to the homes and studios of local artists and artisans working in a wide range of media. Sierra Art Trails features painting, photography, jewelry, sculpture, fiber arts, woodcarving, ceramics, glass, and more. For information visit their website: www.SierraArtTrails.org.

Tarantula Festival – Coarsegold honors the arachnid that migrates around here every fall. Taking place in Coarsegold Historic Village, this spooky and fun event includes food, games, costume contests for the kids, scream contest, hairy leg contest, and of course, tarantula races!

Jerseydale Ranch Pumpkin Patch – Free parking and free admission to this farm with dozens of varieties of pumpkins, squash and gourds. They host games for the kids and photo ops with baby goats. Visitors are also welcome to bring food and have a picnic on site. You may even see an artist or two on site painting the beautiful vistas! Located in Mariposa. Note: the pumpkin patch may be affected by seasonal drought.

Halloween - Families from all around the area flock to the Goldside neighborhood in Oakhurst, off of Highway 49, to trick-or-treat. It's one of the few neighborhoods where houses are closer together, so walking door-to-door is not a huge trek. Arrive early (before the sun goes down) to procure a good parking spot. In addition to Goldside, local churches, the college and some community businesses sponsor a handful of fun, safe, sanctioned "trunk 'n treats." They gather cars together, decorate them for the holiday, and open their trunks filled with assortments of candy.

WINTER

Small Business Saturday – Designated as the Saturday after Thanksgiving, SBS is a great opportunity to support the local small merchants in our community.

Holiday Events – Oakhurst holds an annual Christmas Tree Auction, where ornately decorated trees are donated by local businesses and auctioned off in a live auction, benefitting the Boys & Girls Club. The evening also includes hors d'oeuvres, drinks, and a silent auction. In addition to the auction, there are many fun holiday events in the mountain area, including local boutiques, the Bass Lake parade of lights, and the annual community Christmas tree lightings in Bass Lake, Coarsegold, North Fork and Oakhurst. Don't be surprised if you see Santa at one of these events, he may just arrive on the back of a fire truck!

Sleigh Rides/Carriage Rides – During the holiday season, The Tenaya Lodge offers sleigh rides in the winter months, providing there is snow on the ground. If not, they bring out their old-fashioned carriage. Fun for families and romantic for couples. For more information and schedules, visit their website at www.TenayaLodge.com.

Best Pizza in Oakhurst – Taste the local fares when all of our pizza-making establishments come together to show off their varieties of pizza for the prize. Sponsored by Kiwanis, the community gathers in January for pizza tasting and football viewing at the Oakhurst Community Center. Proceeds go to a designated charitable organization.

MOSTLY YEAR 'ROUND

Madera Wine Trail – Three times a year (February, May, and November) the local wineries participate in this weekend event where they open the doors to the public. Visitors get a map of the wineries participating and have the opportunity to travel at their own pace to visit the tasting rooms of the participating wineries. If you want to drink without a designated driver, Discover Yosemite Tours offers a bus tour that includes transportation from Oakhurst and lunch. For more information visit MaderaWineTrail.com and YosemiteTours.com.

Over 21 - Aside from the wine trails, there is year-round beer tasting at South Gate Brewing Company, wine tasting at our local Idle Hour winery, and even whiskey tasting at

Yosemite Gateway Restaurant. Make sure to bring your IDs!

Yosemite Mountain Sugar Pine Railroad – From March to November, weather permitting, the Yosemite Sugar Pine Railroad takes you back to the logging days with a train ride through the forests of Fish Camp. Their Moonlight Special includes a campfire stop, storytelling and barbecue. Located at 56001 Hwy 41, you must make reservations by calling (559) 683-7273 or purchase your tickets online at www.ymsprr.com.

Fundraising Dinners/Breakfasts – There are so many service, student, and sports organizations in the area, you'll likely find an inexpensive community fundraiser meal at any given time, including frequent drive-throughs. Just check the signs at the corner of Highways 41 and 426 and you'll find announcements for regular barbecues, dinners, breakfasts and food-fests galore.

H.O.W. Dinners - The Oakhurst Chapter of Helping One Woman (HOW) honors and benefits a woman in the community that has suffered a loss or hardship. Anyone can attend, with a small cash gift for entry that benefits the honoree, and each person purchases his/her own meal. . The dinners take place at a designated restaurant on the third Wednesday of the month. For more information, visit www.HelpingOneWoman.org.

Local Workshops - Writing, ukulele, jewelry making, quilting, paint night, you name it! Check the local community calendars for classes in just about anything you can imagine.

Marathons And Triathlons – If you're a runner, there are several marathons in the area that take place annually. In September, the Smokey Bear Run happens at Bass Lake and includes Kids' Races (1/8 mile, 1/4 mile, 1/2 mile), a 2 Mile

Run/Walk, and the big 10k Run. More info can be found on www.smokeybearrun.com. Also in the area are the Bass Lake/Yosemite Triathlon at the beginning of summer, the "My-Tri" Triathlon for youngsters (also at Bass Lake), and the Yosemite Half Marathon around October. More events are added every year.

Golf Clinics & Tournaments – There are two golf courses in the mountain area: River Creek Golf Course in Ahwahnee, and Yosemite Lakes Park Golf Course in YLP. Each course offers recreational golf and holds tournaments and special events throughout the year.

Craft Fairs, Quilting Fair – Throughout the year and especially at the holidays, the mountain town crafters will display and sell their goods through small presentations and fairs. Check any community calendar for these events.

Library Programs – The local branches of the Madera County Library in Oakhurst and North Fork offer many programs for the community. For kids and teens, they present a summer program with free gaming, reading program, writing workshop, and art classes. The libraries offer informational programs and book sales, including collectibles for adults. For more information check out the library calendar for Oakhurst Branch at the Madera County website: www.maderacountylibrary.org.

Coolwater Ranch Concerts – Robin Ralston's Coolwater Ranch off of Road 601 in Nipinnawasse is internationally known for its house concerts, hosting some of the best folk, country, jazz, blues, and multi-genre musicians. In a cozy, intimate atmosphere, you can enjoy an evening of food, drink and entertainment. For more information visit www.coolwaterconcerts.com.

Fresno Flats Historical Village and Park – This park, consisting of historic cabins and homes from the area, recreates life in the 19th century. Two houses, a museum, print shop, jail, gazebo, and schoolhouse can be seen on a self-guided tour or with a docent. The park is maintained and preserved by a group of volunteers and donations. The village and grounds are open daily with the exception of the early months of the year, as weather permits. The park and facilities can also be rented out for parties and events. For more information call (559) 683-6570 or visit their website at www.FresnoFlatsMuseum.org.

Ahwahnee Hills Regional Park – The Ahwahnee Hills Regional Park is a 400-acre nature park just off of Highway 49. It offers five miles of pedestrian hiking trails as well as two miles of equestrian trails. You may walk dogs in the park, as long as they are on a leash and you clean up after them. There are picnic areas, a lake, full restrooms, and a nature study center on site. Entry is free for individuals, but events and reservations require a fee. The park is open Wednesday through Sunday from 8:00 a.m. until dusk. For more information visit www.AhwahneePark.org.

Golden Chain Theatre – Our local non-profit community theater offering wonderful plays, melodramas and musicals throughout the year. Founded in 1967, it puts on both classic and original works. The theater is handicapped-accessible and hosts a full-service saloon offering a variety of drinks, and sometimes informal food and snack options. Located on the north side of town in Oakhurst, at 42130 Hwy 41. For more information visit www.GoldenChainTheatre.org.

Art Galleries at Gallery Row – There are many talented artists in the Yosemite area towns and you can view or purchase their work. Gallery Row in Oakhurst is open regular business hours and also is a main hub in the annual

Sierra Art Trails. Gallery row is located on the north side of Oakhurst at 40982 Highway 41 on the west side of the highway. In North Fork, check out the Greater North Fork Art Gallery and The Studio. For more information visit www.YosemiteGatewayGalleryRow.com.

Bingo – The Sierra Senior Center, behind the Oakhurst Community Center, hosts regular bingo events for the community. And believe it or not, McDonald's on Highway 41 has Wednesday morning bingo where participants get bonus coupons for items like free ice cream and french fries.

Highland Downs Cottage Garden Farm - If you're looking for a local place to purchase organic eggs, breads, pies, produce and other foodstuffs, check out the farm located at 44792 Road 628 in Ahwahnee. Their on-site general store contains homemade canned goods, quilts, and even some antiques. They also offer farm tours and berry/apple picking in the summer months. Plans are to put a pizza eatery on the patio in the future.

Oakhurst Community Park – With a big field and play equipment for kids, the Oakhurst Community Park is a great place for families and pets. The park hosts many local events including classic car shows, the Fall Festival, concerts, and the annual Pet Faire. The park is hidden behind the Oakhurst Branch Library, across a river bridge. It closes at dusk.

Chukchansi Gold Resort & Casino – The casino off of Highway 41 in Coarsegold offers slots, gaming tables, a buffet, a variety of restaurants, bars, the Serenity Springs spa, and hotel rooms. The resort also holds outdoor summer concerts with top music headliners and is a great getaway for locals as well as tourists. For more information visit www.ChukchansiGold.com. 711 Lucky Lane, Coarsegold.

Jones Store – Up Beasore Road off Road 222 in Bass Lake, there is a small general store and eatery called Jones Store. What's unique about this establishment is that it's run completely off the grid with no electricity, no internet...not even a landline phone. Mr. and Mrs. Jones (well into their 90's) have a preselected menu for diners each day that usually includes burgers and beer. Located in Beasore Meadow, they offer cabins for rent, a hearty meal, camping supplies and sometimes even gas. Don't leave without tasting Lois Jones' delicious home-made pie. On the way to or from Jones Store, make a point to stop at Globe Rock, an unusually balanced boulder that makes an excellent photo-op!

Globe Rock on Beasore Road

Dining Out - There are a multitude of notable eateries here in the mountain towns, everything from casual to elegant, from breakfast to burgers to steak to vegan cuisine. There are so many great restaurants we can't list them all, but check out yelp.com or a little publication called *Mountain Menus & More,* found in most grocery stores.

CLASSES FOR MANY INTERESTS

If you want to take a class to expand your knowledge or improve your skills, you'll have plenty of opportunity to do so here in the mountains. Want art classes? Pak 'n Page, Just Bisque It, and The Cat's Meow are just some of the local favorites for crafting. Looking for a professional artist to guide you in a creative direction? There's a very active group operating under the umbrella of Western Sierra Artists. Kids and adults can take dance lessons, and for those who like a western twist on their twinkle toes, there's Line and Square Dancing. Fancy sewing by the fireside or under a shady tree? Stop in at Bear Paw Quilts on Highway 41 in Oakhurst, or if you're interested in learning to work with wood, contact the California Carvers Guild and make note of their annual destination convention, the Woodcarvers' Rendezvous. Visit Oakhurst's Carvers Guild page for more information: www.cacarversguild.org.

MUSEUMS

If you're interested in the history of the Yosemite area, its inhabitants, culture, or environment, you can visit the many museums in the area. From trees to treasures, there is a museum for every interest.

Ansel Adams Gallery – Yosemite Valley, YNP
www.anseladams.com

Consortium of Southern Yosemite Museums
www.southyosemitemuseums.org

California State Mining and Mineral Museum - Mariposa
www.camineralmuseum.com

Children's Museum of the Sierra – Oakhurst
www.childrensmuseumofthesierra.com

Coarsegold Historic Museum - Coarsegold
www.coarsegoldhistoricalsociety.com

Fresno Flats' Laramore-Lyman House - Oakhurst
www.fresnoflatsmuseum.org

Friends of Nelder Grove – Oakhurst
www.neldergrove.org

Happy Isles Nature Center – Yosemite Valley, YNP
www.nps.gov/yose/planyourvisit/historic.htm

Little Church on the Hill - Oakhurst
www.southyosemitemuseums.org/lcoh

The Pioneer Yosemite History Center – Wawona
www.nps.gov/yose/planyourvisit/upload/pyhc.pdf

Raymond Museum & Historic Town Site - Raymond
www.southyosemitemuseums.org/rm

Sierra Mono Museum – North Fork
www.sierramonomuseum.org

Thornberry Museum at the Yosemite Mountain Sugar Pine Railroad – Fish Camp
www.ymsprr.com

Yosemite Museum – Yosemite Valley, YNP
www.nps.gov/yose/learn/historyculture/yosemite-museum.htm

GARDENING, DAY TRIPS, & KID STUFF

For those who are passionate about gardening or just want to start a window box, check out the University of California Master Gardeners who get their hands dirty here in Madera County. Their mission is to help local gardeners and provide free workshops, as does True Value in Oakhurst.

Western Sierra Nursery on Golden Oak Drive carries plants, trees, gardening supplies and gifts, and Mountain Feed and Nursery in Coarsegold has supplies for garden, pets and livestock – since your mountain garden may even grow to include chickens and other creatures formerly thought of as farm animals. For instance, many have traded a love of shoe shopping for chicken-tending and, fortunately, there are friendly "support" groups for that fascination, online. Try Mountain Chicken Chicks on Facebook, where roosters are welcome, too. Check out Sue Langley's local gardening blog, SierraFoothillGarden.com, offering advice and tips on working with our native plants and flowers.

Day trip opportunities abound, as pretty much every direction you head in any season will take you someplace wonderful. If you're the type of person who likes to read historic markers, you've hit the jackpot, since the museums, interpretive centers and historical societies in this area will give you plenty to discover when it comes to local history. *The Ancient and Honorable Order of E Clampus Vitus* is a fraternal organization dedicated to the study and preservation of the gold mining regions of the American West. These "Clampers" have erected beautiful granite markers at various local historical sites in our area, adding more every year. For more information, visit www.eclampusvitus.com.

...OR JUST TAKE IT EASY

When you move to the mountains, you might watch the clock less and pay more attention to the sunrise and sunset. Life slows down a little and you could find yourself more at peace and communing with nature. It sounds corny, but it's true.

Time once spent somewhat frantically running errands, taking meetings and driving endlessly on urban freeways becomes devoted to simply relaxing and enjoying the beautiful vistas that surround you. Being in nature is no longer something you do on the weekend, but an activity you can enjoy every day. So for starters, go where the day and trails take you.

Fishing at Bass Lake

Each season arrives with its own to-do list. The scent of wildflowers comes from all directions in spring just as the earth breaks into a bright, omnipresent green and nighttime brings the sounds of incessant croaking and chirping. Your activities could range from gardening to just chilling on the deck to absorb the rapidly changing scenery.

As the daily heat of summer cools to warm, breezy nights, priorities could shift to planning a hike or paddle on the next full moon or staying out all night to watch a meteor shower. It's lemonade season, made from scratch because you stand in front of a window, looking out while you squeeze the fruit. You watch leaves drop in the fall, as the sunsets grow increasingly psychedelic in color, and finally you gaze at the gentle rain or snowfall of winter, comfy in front of your wood stove, before doing it all over again. When all else fails? Take a well-deserved nap.

CHAPTER 6
Minding Your Business

As you can imagine, many people in the Yosemite mountain communities work in the sales and tourist trades. There are a multitude of hotels, restaurants, and attractions in and surrounding the national park that provide work for many of the residents. The Chukchansi Gold Resort & Casino, alone, employs close to a thousand people managing and maintaining the gaming, restaurants, hotel and special events. Our local communications company, Sierra Tel, and the public school system are also among the largest employers in the area.

14% of the mountain town residents work in public service (law enforcement, firefighting, schools, and county supervision). Construction is a popular occupation, now that the housing market has picked up again. It seems our mountain towns have at least "one of everything," so if you're looking for a chiropractor, a web designer, a massage therapist, dentist, or handyman, there will be someone who can get the job done.

STARTING OR MOVING YOUR BUSINESS

There are many opportunities for business owners in the Yosemite mountain towns, and yet there are drawbacks, too. The best thing you can do for your new business is to join one of the Chambers of Commerce. There are four in the area, depending on the location of your business: Oakhurst, Coarsegold, Bass Lake, and North Fork. The Chambers are wonderful resources to research the history of businesses that have thrived here and those that have not. They also provide directories, networking, and events where you can connect with other business owners in the area. As far as membership fees, the Oakhurst Chamber is affordable for even the small businessperson. They also offer a monthly payment plan, so you don't have to pay your yearly fees up front.

The most important piece of advice for a new or existing business moving to the area is to do your research. Our small community is very different than hanging up a shingle in a big city, and there have been many businesses that have tried and failed because they hadn't learned about the local market before opening their doors.

> I moved to the mountains in the beginning of 2015. What surprised me the most is how well my business is going now! *–Anthony G.*

If you're interested in opening a retail store, check with the appropriate chamber on the types of shops that thrived previously in the different parts of town. Retail space is fairly inexpensive in our area compared to the city, and it's very tempting to open up that little shop that you've always dreamed about. Unfortunately, many people do so without any retail experience and little business knowledge. Those little shops come and go because the new proprietor didn't understand the tourist market vs. local, or foot traffic vs.

drive-by. They didn't take into account the advertising expenses or website costs, competitive analysis, or time for social marketing and in-person networking. We don't live in an "if-you-build-it-they-will-come" society anymore. Not even in a small community.

Historic Mural on the Coarsegold Market

Several years ago our local movie theater closed because they could not remain profitable—even though they were the only theater in town. The Met Cinema was saved by three local filmmakers who bought the business and created a new payment model. For a subscription fee of $19.95 per month, moviegoers can attend as many movies as they want. The new owners figured that if they signed up at least 3,000 subscribers within the community the theaters could succeed. And they did! Matt Sconce, Keith Walker, and James Nelson did their research, calculated their costs and created a business model that would enable the Met Cinema to thrive within the community. It was so successful that the owners have since helped theaters in other communities achieve success with the same revenue model.

Location sharing has also worked within our community to help keep overhead down. Some thrift shops and antique stores offer spaces to rent, which is a great way to display your wares in a corner of a store rather than incurring the expenses of a full retail space.

As far as professional occupations, our community is always in need of accounting, legal, insurance, medical, and other types of personal and business-to-business services.

With the popularity of vacation rental websites, some residents have started businesses renting out extra rooms or entire homes. Many visiting families prefer renting out a home rather than trying to cram into a hotel room or having to pay for several hotel rooms, which can get pricey during the tourist season. Locals have used sites such as AirBNB.com and VRBO.com so successfully that they are now doing it full-time and buying additional real estate just for that purpose.

Although renting out a vacation home seems like a quick and easy way to gain additional income, you will still be running a full-fledged business. It's important to keep proper books, register with the county, pay your taxes, and take into account overhead expenses like electric, gas, cleaning fees, property damage, and extra insurance. You also have to determine whether you will be doing the housekeeping yourself or hiring an individual or company to maintain your rental properties.

Madera County requires a business license and has strict regulations on vacation rentals, so make sure you do it right and follow the rules. County regulators pore over the vacation rental websites regularly, and if you are caught providing the service without going through the proper channels, you will be taxed and possibly fined. Call Madera

County for more information on vacation rental regulations, the transient occupancy tax and required fees: www.madera-county.com/hotel-a-motel-room-tax.

NETWORKING

There are several ways to network as a business person in the community. For women, the combined chambers have a sub-organization called Women In Business (WIB). WIB members meet once a month on the second Thursday for lunch in various locations. Many business leaders also join the multitude of community service organizations, listed in Chapter 4. Volunteering is a great way to get involved with the community as well as getting your business noticed.

Many of the local festivals and events provide booths for business marketing. Whether you're promoting your homemade jam or selling insurance, for a small fee you can rent a tent at any of the seasonal events. In addition, almost every charitable event hosts a silent auction table, and the sponsors are always happy to have local businesses donate baskets or gift certificates for promotion.

THE CHAMBERS OF COMMERCE

Bass Lake: www.BassLakeChamber.com

Coarsegold: www.CoarsegoldChamberofCommerce.com

North Fork: www.NorthForkVisitorCenter.wordpress.com

Oakhurst: www.OakhurstChamber.com

Madera County: www.MaderaChamber.com

CHAPTER 7
Getting Around

The easiest way to get around in the Yosemite communities is by car. Driving around the mountain towns, you'll often find yourself cruising one of the two main highways in the area: California State Route 41 (Southern Yosemite Highway) and California State Route 49 (Golden Chain Highway).

Because a lot of visitors take these roads to and from Yosemite National Park, it's always wise to be extra cautious while driving. Visitors who are not used to the area have been known to drift out of their lane while taking in our spectacular views. Some have made sudden U-turns when they've found themselves going down the wrong road. No matter how comfortable you are with our mountain roads, please stay alert and keep your eyes on the road at all times.

ALL WHEEL DRIVE VS. CHAINS

When we get severe snowfall, there are certain places that require either chains or a vehicle with four-wheel or all-wheel drive. At the very minimum, drivers are required to carry tire chains during the winter months.

If you've been looking for an excuse to get yourself an all-wheel-drive vehicle, moving to the mountains could be it. While it's not mandatory to have a car that can operate efficiently in foul weather, there are almost always a few times of year when it really helps. During rainy episodes, a rugged ride helps navigate the rocky and sometimes rock-sliding terrain of the area, and when it does snow, the added control and safety of a an all-wheel-drive or four-wheel-drive are considered highly desirable. Most of the snowfall below 5,000 feet will only accumulate to a few inches and usually melts away in a day or so, sometimes well before you even want it to go. You may never need your 4x4 but if snowfall persists in town or you plan to go into the higher country, it's a tremendous convenience and can be a literal lifesaver.

In the meantime, it's always recommended that drivers in the mountains carry tire chains that fit their vehicle, and occasionally chains are required during the snowy season before you reach the snowline. Chains are easy to purchase at an average of $25 per vehicle, however not so easy to install, depending who and where you are. If you're comfortable putting chains on your car, that's great—you are one step ahead. If the act of securing chains on tires is not something you expect to ever accomplish in your lifetime, keep $20 or more dollars in your glove box for emergencies: chances are, where there are CHP Chain Control Alerts, there are hearty souls who will assist you for a fee.

RIDES

There are certainly alternative methods of transportation in the mountains, including person-to-person rideshare services, one taxi, and several public transportation systems.

Taxi - Rosemarie Wright is the owner of the Starlight Taxi (CA License Bo102242), and is available from 8 a.m. to 10 p.m. seven days a week, with earlier and later rides available by appointment. Starlight most often transports riders between Oakhurst and Coarsegold, to the Fresno airport, Amtrak/Greyhound station, and has even gone as far as the San Francisco airport as a special request. For more information or to request a ride, call (559) 641-6641.

Person-to-Person Ride Services – Although Uber and Lyft are thriving in the bigger cities, they're still fairly new to our mountain communities. We have several residents who drive for these ride servies, with the ability to take you as far as Fresno, Mariposa and the city of Madera. To hail an Uber or Lyft, you download the app to your smart phone, sign up, and enter your payment information. All the money is transacted over the app, and because these drivers get premium rates, you don't have to tip them. As the community becomes more technology-enabled, the person-to-person ride services will become more popular and more drivers will get certified in the area.

YARTS - Yosemite Area Regional Transportation System, or YARTS for short, is a public bus system that has four routes, one of which goes from Fresno to Yosemite National Parks with stops at the Park & Ride at State Highway 145, Chukchansi Casino, Coarsegold, Oakhurst, Tenaya Lodge, Wawona Hotel, and various stops in the Yosemite Valley. In Fresno, the stops are at Kaiser Permanente, Fresno State University, Fresno International Airport, and the Amtrak Train/Greyhound Stations. The YARTS bus is currently seasonal. For more information and to view the detailed schedule, visit www.yarts.com.

Mountain Shuttle – The family that owns Photo Safari Yosemite also offers a shuttle service around the mountain area and to Fresno. It is a flat-fee service, which they say is less expensive than taking a cab to or from Fresno. Mountain Shuttle is not a car service by legal definition, but they are considered a charter transport. For quotes and availability call Patrick Althizer at (559) 760-6124.

Senior Transport – The Madera County Community Action Partnership provides rides for seniors 60 years and older as well as disabled persons. They cover Oakhurst, Bass Lake, Coarsegold and Ahwahnee. Ride reservations must be made 24 hours in advance. For more information call (559) 673-9173 or visit www.maderacap.org.

Madera County Connection Bus

Madera County Connection – Madera County operates this bus connecting the cities of Coarsegold, Oakhurst, Bass Lake, and North Fork to Chukchansi Casino and Yosemite Lakes Park. The bus runs weekdays from 6:00 a.m. to 8:00 p.m. As of this writing, the fare is $2.00 a ride or $40 for a monthly pass, and children under age five ride free. The MCC bus now stops at the Best Western Hotel in Oakhurst, allowing riders to connect with the YARTS buses, listed above. For the exact route and stops visit their website: bit.ly/maderacc.

Eastern Madera County Senior Bus – The Eastern Madera County Senior Bus is a passenger van provided by the Madera County Transportation Commission and the Oakhurst Sierra Sunrise Rotary Club. It runs weekdays connecting Oakhurst, Coarsegold, Bass Lake and Ahwahnee. As of this writing, the fare is $1.50 for seniors and people with disabilities. For information visit www.maderactc.org.

CHAPTER 8
Health & Wellness

When you move from a well-populated area to the rural foothills of California, you will find a difference in healthcare options. In rural communities such as ours, there just aren't that many doctors, and when one doctor retires or leaves a practice, it's a notable departure with possible repercussions if he or she is not quickly replaced.

If you're a person enjoying reasonably good health, our system may be just fine to service your needs. It's even possible your health will improve with greater access to an outdoor lifestyle. On the other hand, if you have certain chronic health issues, or are currently undergoing treatment such as chemotherapy, radiation, or dialysis, the options here in the mountains may not be suitable for you at this time. Even someone with extreme reactions to allergies or elevation may want to avoid settling around these parts.

When it comes to health care providers in the foothills, the options are relatively limited to a few practices and one Kaiser Permanente facility in Oakhurst. Mariposa has a regional hospital, John C. Fremont, and there are major medical centers in Fresno and Clovis, about an hour's drive from Oakhurst.

The upside of going to a smaller medical practice is that you will probably get to know your doctor, nurses and nurse practitioner quite well, and they'll have the opportunity to get to know you and your medical history. It's not exactly *Dr. Quinn, Medicine Woman*, but it's better than being a random ID number on a file.

ALTERNATIVE MEDICINE

In addition to standard family practice medical care, our mountain towns offer alternative healing practices including chiropractors, acupuncture, cranial-sacral therapy, massage therapists, energy healers, an herbalist, and more. Ask around for a referral if you'd like a reliable local practitioner.

These days, alternative medicine also may include access to medicinal marijuana. According to current Madera County ordinances, which are subject to change, limited amounts of medicinal marijuana are currently legal to grow in small indoor areas and enclosed outdoor areas. However marijuana dispensaries are currently *illegal* in Madera County.

URGENT CARE

Options are limited when it comes to emergency care, as we do not have a 24-hour medical care provider. Adventist Community Health Care is open in Oakhurst seven days a week for non-life-threatening urgent medical needs. They take most major medical plans including Medicare and Medi-Cal, and also offer a discount program for uninsured patients.

Services include family practice, psychology, X-ray, mammography, ultrasound, and laboratory. The clinic located at 48677 Victoria Lane in Oakhurst. It's open Monday through Friday from 8:00 a.m. to 5:00 p.m. and on weekends from 9:00 a.m. to 7:00 p.m.

EMERGENCY SERVICES

In the event of an emergency, you have two options: drive to a hospital or call 911. Depending on the nature of the emergency, a 911 call is dispatched to an ambulance or critical response unit nearby, and responders will come to your aid as soon as possible, from wherever they are in the far-flung foothills. Calls go out all day long for medical aid, with a limited number of responders challenged by a vast response area. In the case of a life or death emergency, a qualified professional will be by your side soon enough to effectively attend to your health.

Sierra Ambulance vehicles

If you do need an ambulance, chances are it will come from Sierra Ambulance, a nonprofit membership model that dates back more than fifty years. The company provides ambulance service to the communities of eastern Madera County, including Oakhurst, Ahwahnee, Bass Lake, North Fork, Coarsegold, Raymond, Fish Camp and O'Neals, along with parts of Yosemite National Park and the Sierra

National Forest. The service was founded in 1964 when residents recognized the need for localized emergency medical aid, and scraped together enough money to buy their own ambulance. Now, with a fleet of state-of-the-art ambulances, members pay $65 annually to support the service and any member of the household is covered for emergency ambulance transportation.

When dispatched, a patient will usually be transported to Fresno whether they have a membership to Sierra Ambulance or not. The difference is that subscribed members are automatically covered for ambulance service, eliminating the need to haggle with insurance or justify the necessity for the ride.

Sierra Ambulance also offers community education and is a ready participant at emergency response and community outreach events. For more information, contact Sierra Ambulance at (559) 642-0650 or visit their website: www.sierraambulance.org.

THE CHAIN OF SURVIVAL

Every first responder in the mountains would likely want you to consider becoming part of the *chain of survival*, a critical design that relies on everyday people being properly trained in lifesaving techniques like CPR and first aid. Each person who is versed in emergency response can help to save a life by pitching in when necessary, in the event of accident or other incident, so the link between life and death remains unbroken while professional teams are on their way to the scene. Local paramedics team Bill and Gina Hartley of Minarets Medical give free CPR and first aid training classes. For more information, you can contact Minarets Medical at (559) 658-1052.

CHAPTER 9
Education and Schools

There's a lot to love about the local schools in Eastern Madera County: caring teachers who are part of the greater community, immediate access to the some of the most abundant landscape on earth, school bus service throughout the area, and distinctive perks like weekly ski sessions at the historic Yosemite Ski and Snowboard Area (formerly Badger Pass).

If your kids are young and you're planning a public education, they will likely attend class in one of three school districts made up of over a dozen primary schools. Alternatively, many students in the mountain area are homeschooled, and some are educated at private academies both religious and secular.

Most of the schools in the area have strong parent-teacher organizations, with engaged parents and supporters who are dedicated to expanding the students' educational opportunities and assist in school fundraising. Parents and supporters are encouraged to help at school dances—often open to multiple schools—and at sporting events. Football is a popular event at both local high schools in the tradition of *Friday Night Lights* and many of the sports from t-ball to water polo are well-attended opportunities for multi-generational community interaction.

From kindergarten through the upper grades, students are exposed to a wide variety of academic challenges as well as the usual regimen of sports being available on a seasonal schedule. Yosemite High School has an outdoor swimming pool that's available for use by students and also the community at large, through Yosemite Marlins Swim Club.

Swim meet at Yosemite High School

HOMESCHOOL

Many families in the mountain area choose to homeschool their children. Aside from the resources available online, Mountain Home School Charter and Glacier High School Charter are available to provide personalized learning that combines the best of homeschool instruction and school-based instruction. For more information visit the Western Sierra Charter School website: www.mountainhomecharter.org.

OTHER EDUCATIONAL OPPORTUNITIES

4-H, which stands for "Head, Heart, Hands, and Health," is a national university-backed youth development program for elementary-aged school children with active chapters in the mountain area. Kids in 4-H learn about everything from livestock to public speaking. With an emphasis on leadership, meetings that are run by 4-H members. 4-H may lead to interest in the high school FFA program (formerly known as Future Farmers of America). Oakhurst has a very popular Boys & Girls Club that helps occupy the kids when school is out and provides excellent activities at an affordable price. For smaller children, there are private preschools, both secular and parochial, as well as state preschools in close proximity to the kindergartens. There's a Head Start program in Oakhurst and also one in North Fork.

There are three school districts in our area: Yosemite Unified, Bass Lake Joint Union Elementary, and Chawanakee Unified. Here is a listing of the schools that belong to each:

YOSEMITE UNIFIED SCHOOL DISTRICT

Rivergold Elementary School, Coarsegold, home of the Hawks (Transitional Kindergarten through 8th grade)

Coarsegold Elementary School, Coarsegold, home of the Cougars (Transitional Kindergarten through 8th grade)

Yosemite High School, Oakhurst, home of the Badgers (grades 9 - 12)

Educational Options Programs, Oakhurst (Evergreen High School)

Yosemite Adult School, and Campbell Community Day School

Website and links to accountability report cards: www.yosemiteusd.com

BASS LAKE JOINT UNION ELEMENTARY SCHOOL DISTRICT

Fresno Flats Day School, Ahwahnee (located on the grounds of Wasuma Elementary)

Wasuma Elementary, Ahwahnee, home of the Wildcats (Transitional Kindergarten through 8th grade)

Oakhurst Elementary, Oakhurst, home of the Eagles (Transitional Kindergarten through 5th grade)

Oak Creek Intermediate, Oakhurst, home of the Coyotes (Middle School grades 6 - 8)

Website and links to accountability report cards: www.basslakeschooldistrict.com

CHAWANAKEE UNIFIED SCHOOL DISTRICT

North Fork Elementary, North Fork, Home of the Cougars (Transitional Kindergarten through 8th grade)

Spring Valley Elementary, O'Neals, home of the Warriors (Transitional Kindergarten through 8th grade)

Minarets High School, O'Neals, home of the Mustangs (Minarets Charter and Minarets International High School, grades 9 - 12)

Mountain Oaks High School, North Fork, home of the Eagles (alternative)

Manzanita and Cougar Springs Community Day Schools, North Fork (opportunity, grades 5 - 12)

Chawanakee Academy, O'Neals, home of the Timberwolves (alternative)

Website and links to accountability report cards: **www.chawanakee.k12.ca.us**.

HIGH SCHOOLS

The mountain towns have two main public high schools: Yosemite High and Minarets High. In addition to traditional high school classes, both school districts also offer alternative educational opportunities as well as adult education classes.

When it comes to the two high schools, it's important as a resident that you know which school your teenager will be eligible to attend, because the schools are very different and transfers can be difficult to attain. Check with the school districts regarding the boundaries in which you live.

Yosemite High School, founded in 1976, offers a modern classroom education experience with many special programs available designed for all academic and social needs. The campus stretches over a hundred acres with about 700 students in attendance as of this writing. Despite its remote rural location, Yosemite High School (YHS) in Oakhurst offers an International Baccalaureate (IB) program, making the school academically unique to the area. The IB Diploma is offered by a nonprofit educational foundation that focuses on intellectual, personal, emotional and social skills needed for students in a globalized world. IB schools must be accredited, and teachers are provided enrichments by the international organization in order to offer kids a rigorous, well-rounded academic experience with an emphasis on language, arts, science, math and critical thinking.

Minarets High School and Charter is south of Coarsegold, off of Road 200 in O'Neals. It is considered a "digital school" and issues an Apple laptop computer to each student for the duration of their enrollment. At Minarets, students are encouraged to live by the six Cs: critical thinking, competency, creativity, collaboration, communication and community, and are taught to chart their own educational path. Established in 2008, the school's emphasis on digital media, arts, performance and self-direction makes Minarets a good option for students looking for an education with a digital focus.

EXTRACURRICULAR TRAINING & ACTIVITIES

Yosemite-adjacent school kids have access to golf, tennis, cheer, soccer, football, basketball, baseball, softball, swim, dive, gymnastics, water polo, wrestling, track, and other staples of a well-rounded athletic program that you'd find in just about any city school. They also have access to sports that are specific to the mountain area, such as archery and equestrian.

If you hear a kid in 5th through 8th grade say they're going to MASS on a Friday, it's probably not church they're talking about, it's Mountain Area Ski School. MASS is a grassroots program dating back to 1961 that today serves about 400 students in elementary and middle school. The staff consists of dozens of instructors, mostly parent and community volunteers, who attend an annual clinic for skiing instructors.

At MASS, students can learn downhill skiing, cross-country skiing and snowboarding, and are bused to Yosemite Ski & Snowboard Area (formerly and still commonly known as Badger Pass, the first-ever ski resort in California) every Friday for approximately twelve weeks, weather permitting. It's an exciting and affordable way for local kids to take advantage of their Yosemite backyard and learn how to ski, with a nominal fee for registration and riding the bus. MASS is also a great way for volunteer parents to connect with the kids. Even if you don't ski, there are still ways to help as a volunteer, like tying boots in the gear room. Bring a few bucks and treat yourself to piping hot French fries while sitting on the deck, taking in the snowy vista. Remember to take sunglasses and sunscreen, as the snow reflects the bright Sierra sun.

Student learning to snowboard at MASS

OAKHURST COMMUNITY COLLEGE

The Oakhurst Community College Center is a local higher learning center, a division of Reedley College. It is the only college in the immediate foothill area, and provides an affordable way to get an Associate Degree, or to complete the credits equivalent to transfer to a four-year university, with guaranteed admission to Fresno State (California State University, Fresno).

The college is housed in six buildings adjacent to the Oakhurst Branch Library, but it's likely to grow larger in the coming years, as Oakhurst is set to receive approximately $25 million dollars from a $425 million dollar bond initiative, which will include improvements to the OCC foothill campus.

OCC provides over 75 courses in a variety of study areas and includes a science classroom and computer lab as well as providing distance learning courses.

CHAPTER 10
Pets & Animal Companions

Homeowners in the mountains adore their animals and it's an ideal place to raise anything from hamsters to mules! There are certainly many pet services available in our communities for your furry family members.

The mountain area communities are blessed with outstanding local vets who provide a tremendous service to the community, often donating time and resources and going the extra mile to save a pet, whether beloved or abandoned.

As of this writing, there are four local veterinary offices located in the area: Oakhurst Veterinary Hospital, Hoof 'N Paw Veterinary Hospital, Coarsegold Veterinary Hospital, and All Things Veterinary Hospital in Bootjack, off of Highway 49 on the way to Mariposa. Yosemite Equine Services and Mariposa Equine Services are available specifically to care for your horses. These vets work regular business hours during the week and are sometimes available on weekends. They provide basic pet care, vaccinations, spay and neutering, and some surgical services.

PET EMERGENCY MEDICAL SERVICES

One important note to pet owners, though, is that there are no emergency veterinary services in the mountain area towns after business hours. The closest pet emergency center is located in northern Fresno, at least a 45-minute drive from the center of Oakhurst, and it's a good idea to familiarize yourself with the options before it becomes necessary:

San Joaquin Vet Hospital
4333 North Blackstone Avenue
Fresno, CA 93726
(559) 500-3787

Fresno Veterinary Specialty and Emergency Center
6606 N Blackstone Avenue
Fresno, CA 93710
(559) 451-0800

Veterinary Emergency Service
1639 N Fresno Street
Fresno, CA 93703
(559) 486-0520

Pet ER
7375 N Palm Bluffs Avenue
Fresno, CA 93711
(559) 437-3766

PET MEDS AND SUPPLIES

Living in the mountains you may encounter pests you've never dealt with before. Among the most rampant of diseases in dogs and sometimes cats is heartworm. Heartworm, or *Dirofilaria immitis*, is a parasitic roundworm that's spread from host to host through the bites of mosquitos. Heartworm can also affect wild animals including coyotes and foxes, but it's most prevalent in dogs, and it's a very sad disease to see take hold. The worms grow to infect the pulmonary system and even veins, and death comes by way of congestive heart failure. The good news is that heartworm is avoidable through a preventative routine of monthly medication. Heartworm medicine is available at local veterinary offices and online. It's important to mark your calendar and never miss a dose, because mosquitoes do not necessarily abide by traditional seasons, and a single bite can transmit disease.

There are several specialty pet and feed stores in the mountain towns that carry most anything for your pet or livestock, from food to meds to hay to even small critters. In addition, the various grocery and hardware stores carry the basic pet food, litter, and accessories.

SPAY AND NEUTER

According to the Humane Society of the United States, approximately 2.4 million healthy, adoptable cats and dogs—about one every 13 seconds—are put down in U.S. shelters each year. Here in the mountains, unfortunately, we get many unwanted pets dumped by irresponsible owners, some who have actually driven all the way from the city to do the nasty deed. They think it's okay to dump an animal in hopes that some kind-hearted animal lover will rescue their unwanted pet or it will miraculously "live in the wild" which most pets cannot.

The only way to reduce the number of abandoned animals is to make sure your four-legged darling is spayed or neutered. For information on low-cost vaccination clinics, contact the Eastern Madera County SPCA (EMC SPCA) and also the Madera County Animal Control offices. Check with the local feed supply stores in Oakhurst who frequently partner with local vets to offer low-cost vaccination and spay/neuter clinics. If you decide to take a pet to one of these affordable clinics, be sure to arrive early as they tend to be very popular.

PET ETIQUETTE

There's a strict leash law in California that says that dogs must be contained to their own yard or be on a leash. The Madera County Sheriff and many residents will not tolerate stray and wandering dogs. In fact, it's within a homeowner's right to shoot any dog that wanders onto their property or poses a potential threat. But we don't want to hurt your loved one, so it is your responsibility to keep your dog confined and safe.

Barking dogs can also create conflict between residents. Continuously barking dogs can and will irritate your neighbors; it's as much a noise nuisance as a loud party or blasting stereo. In fact, a dog owner can be cited by law enforcement if their dog is barking for more than twenty minutes, as it is considered disturbing the peace.

Also, constant barking is a sign of distress. To combat this, don't leave your dog outdoors for hours at a time, or when you're not at home, or overnight. If your dog has a barking problem, consider hiring one of the several local dog trainers to help you improve your pal's behavior and stress level.

PET SAFETY

If you have a small pet such as a cat or little dog, and you want to keep them alive, keep them indoors or outside on a leash. Predators come in many forms in the mountains, and when small animals go missing the usual suspects include coyote, fox, bobcat, sometimes bear and even mountain lion. While many people have "indoor" and "outdoor" cats, the only cat with sustainable longevity in the mountains is going to be those that stay indoors. Even small dogs can—and have been—carried away by large birds of prey. The forest is full of creatures that could easily consider your pet their next meal.

Summer can host many days in the 90's and 100's in the mountain towns, and therefore it is not advisable to let a dog outside for an extended amount of time without shelter from the sun and an adequate water supply. People will respond to dogs left in cars during the summer season. Leave the pooch at home on hot days. If you don't, you risk your dog's life, and it is not unusual for some good Samaritan to break a car window or call the Sheriff to report dogs trapped in hot cars.

ALONG FOR THE RIDE

There are a handful of establishments that will let dogs accompany you while you shop. Oakhurst Feed & Pet Supply welcome your pups on a leash, but be aware they have several free-roaming cats in residence and a very accessible bunny habitat. True Value will also let you bring your pup inside, either on a leash or in the cart, for smaller dogs. They may even offer a treat at checkout.

Speaking of treats, a couple of drive-throughs around town love dogs and are prepared to give your canine companion something special, if they spot your furry pal riding shotgun. From a sausage or bacon at Pete's to a puppuccino (whipped cream in a disposable cup) at Starbucks, your dog will soon start licking his lips when you pull up to one of these drive-through windows.

Conversely, there are some establishments that have their own pets in residence and so it's best that you don't bring yours with you. For example, Sullivan's Tire Pros has two Labs who might greet you at the door and make sure the shop is running smoothly. At Bodys by Boyd you might encounter Shinala, a half-wolf canine who is more gentle than she appears. Some stores have cats in residence, as well.

Area resident enjoys a puppucino

Be aware that many trails in Yosemite National Park do not allow pets. Check their website ahead of time so that you don't have to leave your furry friend in the car for any extended period of time.

If you are taking a trip without your pet, there are many competent pet sitters and boarding kennels in the area. Most of them require your pets to have proof of current vaccinations. Make sure to procure an immunization record from your veterinarian before you drop off your pet, or they could turn you away at the door.

ANIMAL CHARITIES, RESCUES & ADOPTION

If you're looking to add a furry member to your family, there are several organizations in the area that can help.

Kellen Rescue provides rescue, rehabilitation and forever-home placement. All of their animals are in foster homes and can be viewed on PetFinder.

The Eastern Madera County SPCA has met its fundraising goal and has broken ground on a permanent no-kill shelter building along Highway 49 in Ahwahnee. Meanwhile, the EMC SPCA still provides adoption services, spay and neuter assistance, low-cost vaccine clinics, a trap and release program, micro-chipping, and a lost and found listing service. In spring, the EMC SPCA hosts the annual "Oakminster Dog Show," an inclusive and informal competition for both mixed breed and purebred pups. As of this writing, the EMC SPCA runs a thrift store on Highway 41 in Oakhurst.

For lost and found dogs, make sure to check out "Mountain Dog Watch," and active Facebook group with thousands of community members. Many a four-legged friend has been returned safely to its family through the vigilant network of online animal lovers. For more information visit www.emcspca.org.

In the case of fire or emergency evacuation, the Central California Animal Disaster Team (CCADT) assists emergency responders and Red Cross with displaced animals, sheltering and reuniting them with their owners. Throughout the year the CCADT offers educational workshops on disaster preparedness for pets. For more information or to volunteer for the team, visit their website at www.ccadt.org.

FARM ANIMALS, LIVESTOCK & HORSES

If you are interested in keeping livestock or farm animals, be aware that it takes food, money, and a commitment to their well-being and safety. However, if you're new to the area and just want eggs or some great grass-fed beef every now and then, it's probably better to make friends with those who do own farm animals. Much less of a commitment and expense.

There are many mountain residents that keep horses on their property or board them at nearby stables. The Yosemite gateway area has a multitude of trails and spots for great riding, but our environment can be challenging to a horse's health. Horse owners must be careful to keep the hay clean and off of the ground, as the granite in our dirt can wreak havoc on an equine digestive system.

Like other farm animals, horses require shelter from the sun and heat, as well as a steady source of water, which is difficult to provide in times of drought. They also need a good amount of acreage for exercise, and regular grooming of their coat and hooves. You also have to consider that there are just a handful of vets here in the foothills that are available and trained to treat larger animals. If you're part of a community or homeowners' association, it's also prudent to check your CC&R's before stocking your ranch. Big animals equal big expense.

It may seem like an idyllic dream to ride your own horse over the hills and through the trails of the mountains, but it takes money, care and commitment to be a horse owner.

CHAPTER 11
Wonders of the Wilderness

From bugs to bears, and poison oak to falling pine trees, living in the wilderness, or even wilderness-adjacent, has steep rewards and sometimes scary challenges.

Aside from the stunning sunsets and glistening snow, one of the first things you'll notice upon your move to the mountains is the wildlife. This closeness to nature may even be one of the reasons you've chosen to live here, and a strong love of wildlife unites most of the area's residents. All creatures great and small have a place in the forest, and sooner or later, each will reveal themselves to you in every changing season, if you're lucky (or in some cases *not* so lucky).

Living in the mountains you'll suddenly encounter creatures you had only previously seen on *Animal Planet*. There's a good chance you'll see a skunk or five, but they primarily come out and wander the land at night. If you own a pet that goes outdoors, you'll want to become close friends with your dog groomer, or have a DIY recipe to get the stink off, as skunks often get spooked by dogs and will give them a healthy spray.

Raccoons are also abundant in the area, and while they may look cute at first glance these ring-tailed terrors are the biggest carriers of disease, according to Yosemite park rangers. Whether rabid nor not, raccoons can be also vicious. *Do not pet.*

Turkey vultures are ever-present in the mountains with lofty wingspans and an insatiable appetite for road kill. You might see them on your property feasting on a dead carcass, or alerting you to one by surfing the air in circles overhead. Other large birds that might come to visit include flocks of actual wild turkeys, peacocks, hawks, osprey, and an occasional blue heron. Eagles have been spotted at Bass Lake and the surrounding towns. Yosemite Audubon is a great club to follow or join if you're thinking bird-watching is on your to-do list.

Listen closely and you'll hear the tock-tock-tock of the intelligent raven, the insistent tapping of woodpeckers as they look for bugs, the evocative cry of the quail, or the gentle "hoo" of the woodland owl. You'll be charmed by hummingbirds and the variety of finches that stop by to take advantage of your thistle seed buffet.

We also have lions, bears, bobcat, coyote, foxes, and occasional roving gangs of wild pigs left over from French farmers who imported them in the late 19th century. And then there are entire seasons where all you hear are frogs, crickets, and cicadas at night.

HELLO, DEER!

Another critter you'll become friendly with, no doubt, is the abundant mule deer. Families of deer are common in the mountains, and some drivers swear that any speed over 30 miles per hour won't give you time to brake for them. Not only can a collision maim or kill these wonderful animals, but it can also cause serious damage to a car and its occupants. So proceed with caution when driving our mountain roads, and especially when navigating blind turns.

Deer are either plentiful or ridiculously plentiful, depending on the neighborhood and number of resident dogs, anxious to scare them away. Deer are charming guests that will eat everything in your garden, with the exception of daffodils and a few other plants that don't taste good to them, that the local nursery can recommend. The easy-going gardener may wish to forego an adversarial relationship with deer by growing most flowers, vegetables and fruit trees inside a deer-proof, fenced area. Whether you fall into the feed-the-deer category or don't-feed-the-deer category depends on if you want to pay for food and attract their predators, or if you feel the tick-carrying deer are better off surviving on their own. A good compromise may be leaving a bucket of water out for all animals to drink from in the hot, dry summer months.

LIONS, SPIDERS, & BEARS, OH MY!

Just when you think you've heard it all, you'll find yourself listening to unrecognizable sounds that go bump in the night, as well as roar, scream, growl, screech, howl and yip. Starting at the top of the food chain of predators, you may become familiar with mountain lions, and bears.

Mountain lion, also known as cougars, are referred to scientifically as *Felis concolor* or *puma concolor*, meaning "cats of one color." They've been roaming the Americas for 40,000 years, and nowadays, the California Department of Fish and Wildlife (CDFW) estimates that there may be one lion for every twenty square miles in these parts. The cougar is plain-colored like the African lion, but with a slighter build, and a head that's smaller in proportion to the body. The tawny cats have dark brown on either side of the muzzle and backs of the ears, with a creamy white coloring on the chin, upper lip, chest and belly. The long, prevalent tail is dark at the tip. Often dogs, at a distance, can be mistaken for mountain lions, and many locals go their entire lives without ever seeing the real thing. However, if you've ever taken a hike in the woods, chances are a mountain lion has seen you.

Generally speaking, there's not too much to fear. According to the Mountain Lion Foundation, the historical odds of someone being fatally mauled by a lion in the United States are about one in a billion. The lion's favorite meal in this region would be deer, of which there are plenty, however mountain lions and other predators will take advantage of all sorts of free-range food.

As stated in the previous chapter, if you plan to have pets or livestock including dogs, cats, chickens, goats, sheep, horses and cattle, get them tucked in at night if you want to see them again in the morning. Many a cat, small dog, goat and other animals have gone missing due to the eclectic tastes of not just mountain lion, but also fox, coyote, bobcat, and even stray dog who sometimes run in small packs through unfenced neighborhoods. The bottom line is, keep your pets close to home and your livestock safely enclosed.

Even though lion attacks on people are rare, you should still take certain precautions while living or recreating in areas with lions, according to the CDFW. Experts recommend that people avoid walking, running or playing alone in low light conditions, and keeping the area around your house well-lit and clear of dense brush. If hiking with children, keep them near you and don't allow them to run on ahead.

Even after living here for years, the mountain lion still remains hidden to many, but the female "scream" is unmistakable, and it can be heard several times a year at mating season. The sound can be terrifying, unless you're safe inside the house. In that case, it's fascinating to hear what's happening outside your window.

Remember what the experts say—when it comes to wildlife of any kind, we're staking a claim in *their* territory, not the other way around. For more information about living in areas with mountain lions visit the CDFW website at www.wildlife.ca.gov.

DON'T FEED THE BEARS

According to the CDFW, the black bear population in California has almost doubled in the last 35 years, with an estimated 20,000 to 30,000 in residence throughout the state. About 40% of the California black bear population live here in the Sierra Nevada range, where experts figure there is one bear for every square mile.

Large-bodied with a small head and powerful limbs, black bears can range in color from tan or brown to black. Adult females weigh between 100 to 200 pounds, and adult males are larger, usually between 150 to 350 pounds. Some individual bears taken by hunters in California have weighed in at over 600 pounds!

If you should find yourself face-to-face with a local bear, experts have the same advice as that for mountain lions: do not run. Running will trigger their predatory instincts, and they're more likely to chase you. Instead, make yourself as big as you can by holding out your arms, and make noise. If you're in or near your home, bang pots, holler, stomp your feet and hold your ground.

A dog is a great asset when hiking in the wilderness. If a dog alerts, chances are there's something out there. It's also helpful to learn to identify the scat and footprints of different mountain animals. Bear scat is chunky and often has berries in it, whereas other predators who are carnivores will leave behind little tufts of fur in their scat.

Nearly everyone you talk to who's lived in the mountains for any length of time has a good bear story. While it's nice on summer nights to keep your windows open, watch for what could be on the other side of that sliding screen. Food left out on your kitchen counter, or even a scented candle on the table, could attract a bear willing to come into your house and see what tastes good. Keep your outside trash locked up if you don't want to clean up after "Yogi" and friends, as well as any refrigerators or freezers in your garage.

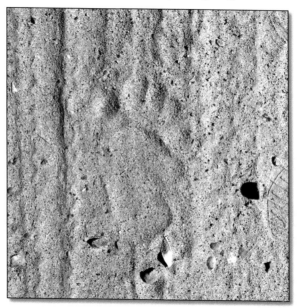

Black bear track

The lesson here is the same in the house as it is in the campground: keep your food put away, and your trash enclosed or otherwise protected.

TARANTULAS AND OTHER CREEPY-CRAWLIES

The first couple of months living in the mountains you might jump out of your skin or let out a blood-curdling scream when you see your first giant spider or caramel-colored scorpion just chilling out on the wall of your bedroom. The longer you live here, the less "creepy" the crawlies become. They are a part of the ecosystem and whether you choose to relocate them outdoors or suck them up into the vacuum, your reaction eventually lessens and your fears calm.

California's native tarantula are usually active in the mid-to-lower elevations of the foothills in the early fall months of September and October, depending on the heat. The watchful eye may spot one as they migrate from their ground dens and move about on the road with their tall, hairy legs. They're hard to miss, as tarantulas can grow to be as large as five inches.

If you see two tarantulas struggling in what appears to be a mighty battle, look away politely: they are probably mating. Most importantly, please do not kill them! Mountain residents have a high regard for these hairy creatures, as they are considered good for the environment and eat bugs. While they're only mildly venomous, these big hairy arachnids rarely bite and are usually safe to handle.

Tarantulas are so common that they have their own festival every fall: The Coarsegold Tarantula Festival. This well-attended appreciation-fest takes place each October, and comes with a wide variety of activities including a screaming competition and (human) hairy-leg contest. The Tarantula Festival always ends with, of course, tarantula races. It's small town living at its creepiest and the festival is both great fun and highly educational.

Spiders are as common as clouds in the mountains, and you'll run into all sorts. Venomous black widows are known to prefer dark places, so use a flashlight when you're poking around at night. Many of the problems associated with bugs can be fixed by chemically treating your home's perimeter. Some homeowners spray insecticide regularly, whereas others prefer to maintain a lifestyle free of chemicals.

Treat yourself to a sturdy, telescoping duster for overall spider web and cobweb maintenance. You'll need it! If you want help eliminating spiders and other unwanted pests, there are a handful of qualified exterminators that serve the Yosemite mountain towns.

MORE BUGS AND CREEPERS

Mosquitos are plentiful in the mountains, especially in and around stagnant pools of water. To counterattack the mosquito population, don't let water deposits stand longer than a day or else larvae may form. Be sure to use bug repellent on humans and regular doses of heartworm medication on pets. Other means of control include outdoor fans (they can't fly in the wind) and citronella-scented candles or citronella incense sticks.

If you see a bat or two "hanging around" your eaves at night, don't fret. These lovely mammals feed on mosquitoes and other buggy insects. As long as the bats stay outside your home, they're harmless and beneficial to keep around. If you're not fond of sweeping up the guano on your doorstep in the morning, consider mounting a designated bat house on a nearby tree or post.

Another fun crawler you'll encounter is the non-threatening praying mantis, which comes in a variety of different sizes and colors—a species that wins the prize for looking most like an alien from another planet.

Indoors, you may fight an army of ants trying to invade your kitchen as weather becomes dry. Outside, wasps will build tiny, strong homes out of mud, some in the ground and some up high around your eaves. Ticks are a pain, particularly in spring and summer when simply taking a walk can lead to wearing small bloodsuckers on your skin. Ticks are known to carry Lyme disease, and a thorough tick-check is warranted after hiking, playing, or dog-walking in grassy areas. That means check under your clothes, in the kids' armpits and other places that tend to be dark and moist, as well as the hair, neck and folds of skin. Be prepared by knowing how to remove ticks safely and effectively, and have necessary tools available.

The creepers that might cause you the most alarm are scorpions, millipedes and multi-colored centipedes. Your previous mental image of a scorpion is probably what you've seen in the movies or on TV: fairly terrifying, dark, and the size of a lobster. Don't fear. Most scorpions in our area are less than an inch long, small and sort of blonde or brown in color. If they do sting you, it is equivalent to a bee sting. Irritating, but not fatal.

Many people take to social media for help to identify the creepy crawlies they encounter on a regular basis. There's also a very handy website, aptly named "What's That Bug: www.Whatsthatbug.com.

Aside from having pages of information on the different types of bugs, you can upload a picture and the community can help identify it for you. You can also search for key words such as gross, huge, hairy, many-legged and no legs.

Our next candidate for most alarming is the millipede, which at first glance may look like a dark rubber band, or a twisted black hair-tie. To this day, it

A standard harmless millipede

can be hard to figure out how they get in the house, but they are frequently found in two positions: curled up tightly wound up in a coil, or casually crawling across the floor as if to say, "Excuse me, pardon me, nothing to see here!"

It's unclear how many species of millipedes exist in California, but the common ones tend to be grey/black in color and large in size at about three inches in length. They're completely harmless and this is a good bug for kids to carefully catch, observe and release, because it won't harm those who aren't afraid to touch it. It helps to keep a jar handy to expedite certain bugs out of the house and back in the garden where they're helpful.

Next on the list of mountain bugs is the carnival of crawlers, the lovely and iridescent, multicolored centipede. You may notice its movement, slithering quickly across the floor, but don't pick up this pretty little thing: it stings.

You are also likely to encounter pumpkin bugs (also called kissing bugs as they attach to one another during mating season), wasps, big ants that bite, little ants that stink, and hopefully a host of honey bees. Even the smallest of species is truly an important part of the ecosystem, and with a little research you may find that your creepy nemesis eventually could become your friend.

THOSE THAT SLITHER

Another reality of living in the woods is the chance that you'll run into snakes and other reptilian characters. The truth is, snakes and lizards are common in the area, but they'll generally stay out of your way unless your loyal hunting pet brings them to you as a gift.

What people really seem concerned about is the possibility of coming face-to-face (or foot-to-fang) with a potentially dangerous species such as the rattlesnake. Depending on where you live, it can happen. Rattlesnakes are more common in the lower elevations, but every resident in the area should be cautious, especially in the warmer months. In order to avoid contact, be aware of shady spots such as woodpiles and larger rocks, and stay on trails and away from tall grass while hiking or walking the dog. If someone is bitten by a venomous creature, call 911 immediately so they can determine how best to get you treated with antivenin which, while effective, is scarce.

As for our canine companions, there is a rattlesnake vaccine that you can have one of the local vets apply to your dog, a great preventative measure that outweighs the cost of the alternative. Rattlesnake aversion training is also available and recommended, depending on your habits, and you can check with your vet or feed store for more information.

WHAT GROWS AROUND COMES AROUND

If you've spent any time in the area at all, you know it's positively resplendent with flowers, plants, and trees. With so much information available on the flora of the foothills, we want to make mention of just a few that stand out.

Buckeye trees here are not the same as some buckeye midwesterners may be familiar with. The local buckeye is the first tree to bud out in late winter and early spring, when other deciduous trees are still bare. Then, when summer has barely arrived, and long before most any other tree or grass goes brown, the buckeye will look as though it has died. Fear not, as the leaves will curl, brown and drop until its little buds sprout again to remind you that spring is around the corner. Beekeepers beware: the buckeye is poisonous to bees and many could die before they learn to avoid it.

A variety of yellow flowers bloom in foothills, and one to watch out for is tar weed. Tar weed gives off a distinctive fragrance, but be careful not to brush up against it as the powdery residue is sticky...and stinky!

Poison oak is abundant and difficult to control without

weed spray. It's also worth noting that poison oak should not be burned, as the spores that cause the rash and itching can literally float through the air and land on unsuspecting people, pets and things. Some people are severely allergic and can even be affected by petting a dog that has run through poison oak. It's said that the spores can survive on fabric such as blankets for months or even years. In the winter, local poison oak drops its leaves and what look like tall sticks arising from the earth are, in fact, spears of discomfort awaiting your touch. Do not pick the stick!

Manzanita bushes and trees are known for their pretty pink petals, and graceful beauty. Many artists are inspired to sculpt, carve and create stunning pieces from the dark brown/red branches of mountain manzanita. You'll see manzanita on your drives, walks, hikes and also your forays into art galleries around the foothills.

Growing daffodils is a delightful way to brighten up the spring garden without tempting the deer: they won't touch it! Planting daffodils in fall and watching as they bloom in spring is one of the many privileges of living in the lower elevations of the Sierra.

Overall, there's such a vast array of flora and fauna in the Sierra that you could probably spend the rest of your life examining, photographing, researching and boasting to your city friends about what lives and grows with you in the mountains. With any luck, that's just what you'll do.

For more information on the animals, flora and fauna in the Yosemite mountain area, visit www.savenature.org, www.wildlife.ca.gov, and www.sierrafoothillgarden.com.

CHAPTER 12
No Regrets

Most of the people who move to the Yosemite mountain area stay here for good. There may be a handful of those who never quite adjust, and some move away to be closer to necessary amenities or family. Those who do stay, though, all have one thing in common: we have no regrets. We love our mountain home and are thankful that we're lucky enough to live here.

We hope that this book has provided all the information and resources necessary for you to make an informed decision to move to the area—or has affirmed your choice to have already settled here. Those of us in the Yosemite gateway towns think our community is pretty special, and we welcome you to join us.

> "Everyone needs beauty as well as bread, places to play in and pray in, where nature may heal and give strength to body and soul." –John Muir

Mountain Glossary

Backcountry: Undeveloped, primitive portions of the area.

Brewery – South Gate Brewing Company restaurant on CA-49 in Oakhurst.

Burn Day – A county mandated day when you can burn for fuel reduction. Depends on air quality and time of year.

Buses – Commercial tour buses carrying a group of tourists, most likely headed to Yosemite National Park.

Car Show – A trophy competition for classic cars.

The Chateau – Erna's Elderberry House and Chateau du Sureau.

Clearing – Removing excess brush and fire hazardous waste from property.

Cruise Night – A gathering of classic car owners for fun and fellowship.

Deadwood – The mountain that separates Oakhurst from Coarsegold. When you travel between those towns you are going "over Deadwood" or "over the hill."

Dog Watch or Mountain Dog Watch – Facebook group for lost and found dogs.

The Flume – Brown's Ditch Flume - a unique hike along metal scaffolding in Bass Lake. Not for those that fear heights.

Gateway Community: A community that exists in close proximity to a unit of the national park system.

Glamping – Glamorous camping, with fancy tents and beds.

Groundwater: Water that exists below the surface of the ground.

Flatlanders – People who are not from the mountain communities, who find it difficult to drive our winding roads.

Hiking the Flume

Hootenanny – a community gathering with folk music and dancing.

Leave No Trace (LNT) – to leave the wilderness as you found it. As the saying goes, "Take only photographs, leave only footprints."

Locals – Full-time residents, as opposed to tourists or seasonal residents.

Lookiloos – People who drive unsafely because they're gazing at the scenic Sierra vistas.

The Met – Subscription-based movie theaters in Oakhurst.

Mountain Time – The phenomenon that causes people to arrive hours late to an appointment.

Natural Quiet: The absence of human-created sounds.

Nelder – Nelder Grove of Giant Sequoias.

Off-Season: Time of year when Yosemite tourism is low, usually from late fall to early spring.

The Park - Yosemite National Park

Peddler's Fair – An antiques and collectibles swap meet in Coarsegold Village every Memorial Day and Labor Day weekend.

Pump – The device that brings water from your well into your reserve tank or house.

Quad - An all-terrain open-air, four-wheel vehicle similar to a motorcycle that can operate on all types of land. Quads usually are trailered to the area in which the riders want to off-road, since they are not allowed on the highways.

Sacred Site – a natural or cultural resource with religious significance to Native Americans, or a locale of private ceremonial activities.

Sierra Cement – Wet sloshy snow in which it's easy to get your vehicle stuck.

Skink – lizard that looks like a snake with legs.

Snow Line – an altitude around 3,000-5,000 feet above which snow and ice cover the ground in winter.

Swamp Cooler – A unit that cools air through the evaporation of water, taking less energy than an air conditioner. Also called an evaporative cooler.

Swap – Mountain Swap Facebook group, or referring to a rendezvous to buy/sell an item initiated online.

Tom – Tom Wheeler, our 5th District County Supervisor.

Tourist Season: Time of year when Yosemite tourism is high, usually from early spring to late fall.

Town – Oakhurst business district converging at Highways 41 and 49. In North Fork, the business district is referred to as "downtown" and in Coarsegold it's "The Village."

Weed Eating/Weed Whacking – Seasonal cutting of the weeds on your property for fuel reduction.

Wood Splitter – a machine that splits tree limbs with the grain to smaller-sized logs for your fireplace.

Whatever-It's-Called-Now – A Yosemite establishment that had to change names because of the new concession contract.

122

Acknowledgments

I would like to thank Carolyn Mather and Melanie Barker for their local expertise and wisdom; Joyce Cortez, the realtor who helped me find my dream home and became my first friend in the mountains; and my darling daughter, Miranda, who provides constant love, optimism and support. *-JM*

I would like to thank Gina Clugston for her invaluable feedback, Virginia Lazar for her talents including photography, and many friends and family whose confidence sustains me, including my sister Jill Flanagan, daughter Clara Briley and husband Dave Briley. *-KF*

About the Authors

Kellie Flanagan is a writer and producer for print, broadcast and web, with credits in all media including short and long-form documentary. Kellie has written and directed for major television and cable networks television shows including *The Wild West, A&E's Biography* and *The Civil War Journal*. As a child actor Kellie played Candace on *The Ghost and Mrs. Muir*, and appeared in the original *Star Trek, The Andy Griffith Show*, and the 60's cult classic film *Wild In The Streets*. Kellie is the Managing Editor of *Sierra News Online*, as well as writer, wife, mom, and chicken-wrangler.

Jennifer Moss is the author of both fiction and non-fiction works. Her book, *The One-in-a-Million Baby Name Book* (Perigee Press) is one of the top books on names and meanings and a companion to her website, BabyNames.com. Her popular series of mystery novels include *Town Red, Way to Go, Taking the Rap*, and *Friend of the Family* (Black Opal Books). Jennifer relocated to Oakhurst in 2011 after surviving 22 years of earthquakes, fires, floods and riots in Los Angeles.

www.LuckytoLiveHereBook.com